Interactive Computing Series

Microsoft® Access 2002 Brief Edition

Kenneth C. Laudon • Robin Pickering

Azimuth Interactive, Inc.

McGraw-Hill
Irwin

Boston   Burr Ridge, IL   Dubuque, IA   Madison, WI   New York   San Francisco   St. Louis
Bangkok   Bogotá   Caracas   Kuala Lumpur   Lisbon   London   Madrid   Mexico City
Milan   Montreal   New Delhi   Santiago   Seoul   Singapore   Sydney   Taipei   Toronto

McGraw-Hill Higher Education

*A Division of The **McGraw-Hill** Companies*

This book is printed on acid-free paper.

1 2 3 4 5 6 7 8 9 0 QPD/QPD 0 9 8 7 6 5 4 3 2 1

ISBN   0-07-247256-1

Publisher: *George Werthman*
Developmental editor I: *Sarah Wood*
Senior marketing manager: *Jeff Parr*
Senior project manager: *Pat Frederickson*
Senior production supervisor: *Michael R. McCormick*
Senior designer: *Pam Verros*
Supplement producer: *Mark Mattson*
Cover photograph: *Bill Brooks/© Masterfile*
Interior design: *Asylum Studios*
Cover designer: *JoAnne Schopler*
Compositor: *Azimuth Interactive, Inc.*
Typeface: *10/12 Times*
Printer: *Quebecor Printing Book Group/Dubuque*

Library of Congress Control Number: 2001093934

www.mhhe.com

InformationTechnology

Information Technology at McGraw-Hill/Irwin

At McGraw-Hill Higher Education, we publish instructional materials targeted at the higher education market. In an effort to expand the tools of higher learning, we publish texts, lab manuals, study guides, testing materials, software, and multimedia products.

At McGraw-Hill/Irwin (a division of McGraw-Hill Higher Education), we realize that technology has created and will continue to create new mediums for professors and students to use in managing resources and communicating information with one another. We strive to provide the most flexible and complete teaching and learning tools available as well as offer solutions to the changing world of teaching and learning.

MCGRAW-HILL/IRWIN IS DEDICATED TO PROVIDING THE TOOLS FOR TODAY'S INSTRUCTORS AND STUDENTS TO SUCCESSFULLY NAVIGATE THE WORLD OF INFORMATION TECHNOLOGY.

- **Seminar series**—Technology Connection seminar series offered across the country every year demonstrates the latest technology products and encourages collaboration among teaching professionals.

- **Osborne/McGraw-Hill**—This division of The McGraw-Hill Companies is known for its best-selling Internet titles: Harley Hahn's Internet & Web Yellow Pages, and the Internet Complete Reference. Osborne offers an additional resource for certification and has strategic publishing relationships with corporations such as Corel Corporation and America Online. For more information visit Osborne at www.osborne.com.

- **Digital solutions**—McGraw-Hill/Irwin is committed to publishing digital solutions. Taking your course online does not have to be a solitary venture, nor does it have to be a difficult one. We offer several solutions that will allow you to enjoy all the benefits of having course material online. For more information visit www.mhhe.com/solutions/index.mhtml.

- **Packaging options**—For more about our discount options, contact your local McGraw-Hill/Irwin Sales representative at 1-800-338-3987 or visit our Web site at www.mhhe.com/it.

Interactive Computing Series

GOALS/PHILOSOPHY

The *Interactive Computing Series* provides you with an illustrated interactive environment for learning software skills using Microsoft Office. The text uses both "hands-on" instruction, supplementary text, and independent exercises to enrich the learning experience.

APPROACH

The *Interactive Computing Series* is the visual interactive way to develop and apply software skills. This skills-based approach coupled with its highly visual, two-page spread design allows the student to focus on a single skill without having to turn the page. A Lesson Goal at the beginning of each lesson prepares the student to apply the skills with a real-world focus. The Quiz and Interactivity sections at the end of each lesson measure the student's understanding of the concepts and skills learned in the two-page spreads and reinforce the skills with additional exercises.

ABOUT THE BOOK

The **Interactive Computing Series** offers *two levels* of instruction. Each level builds upon the previous level.

Brief lab manual—covers the basics of the application, contains two to four chapters.

Introductory lab manual—includes the material in the Brief textbook plus two to four additional chapters. The Introductory lab manuals prepare students for the *Microsoft Office User Specialist Proficiency Exam (MOUS Certification)*.

Each lesson is divided into a number of Skills. Each **Skill** is first explained at the top of the page in the Concept. Each **Concept** is a concise description of why the Skill is useful and where it is commonly used. Each **Step (Do It!)** contains the instructions on how to complete the Skill. The appearance of the **MOUS Skill** icon on a Skill page indicates that the Skill contains instruction in at least one of the required MOUS objectives for the relevant exam. Though the icons appear in the Brief manuals as well as the Introductory manuals, only the Introductory manuals may be used in preparation for MOUS Certification.

Figure 1

Skill: Each lesson is divided into a number of specific skills

Concept: A concise description of why the skill is useful and when it is commonly used

Do It!: Step-by-step directions show you how to use the skill in a real-world scenario

Hot Tips: Icons introduce helpful hints or trouble-shooting tips

More: Provides in-depth information about the skill and related features

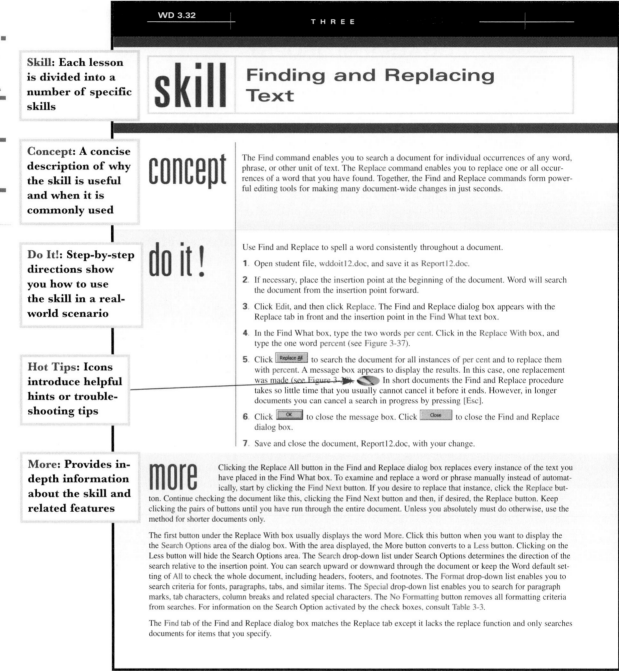

WD 3.32   THREE

skill   Finding and Replacing Text

concept

The Find command enables you to search a document for individual occurrences of any word, phrase, or other unit of text. The Replace command enables you to replace one or all occurrences of a word that you have found. Together, the Find and Replace commands form powerful editing tools for making many document-wide changes in just seconds.

do it !

Use Find and Replace to spell a word consistently throughout a document.

1. Open student file, wddoit12.doc, and save it as Report12.doc.

2. If necessary, place the insertion point at the beginning of the document. Word will search the document from the insertion point forward.

3. Click Edit, and then click Replace. The Find and Replace dialog box appears with the Replace tab in front and the insertion point in the Find What text box.

4. In the Find What box, type the two words per cent. Click in the Replace With box, and type the one word percent (see Figure 3-37).

5. Click Replace All to search the document for all instances of per cent and to replace them with percent. A message box appears to display the results. In this case, one replacement was made (see Figure 3-38). In short documents the Find and Replace procedure takes so little time that you usually cannot cancel it before it ends. However, in longer documents you can cancel a search in progress by pressing [Esc].

6. Click OK to close the message box. Click Close to close the Find and Replace dialog box.

7. Save and close the document, Report12.doc, with your change.

more

Clicking the Replace All button in the Find and Replace dialog box replaces every instance of the text you have placed in the Find What box. To examine and replace a word or phrase manually instead of automatically, start by clicking the Find Next button. If you desire to replace that instance, click the Replace button. Continue checking the document like this, clicking the Find Next button and then, if desired, the Replace button. Keep clicking the pairs of buttons until you have run through the entire document. Unless you absolutely must do otherwise, use the method for shorter documents only.

The first button under the Replace With box usually displays the word More. Click this button when you want to display the the Search Options area of the dialog box. With the area displayed, the More button converts to a Less button. Clicking on the Less button will hide the Search Options area. The Search drop-down list under Search Options determines the direction of the search relative to the insertion point. You can search upward or downward through the document or keep the Word default setting of All to check the whole document, including headers, footers, and footnotes. The Format drop-down list enables you to search criteria for fonts, paragraphs, tabs, and similar items. The Special drop-down list enables you to search for paragraph marks, tab characters, column breaks and related special characters. The No Formatting button removes all formatting criteria from searches. For information on the Search Option activated by the check boxes, consult Table 3-3.

The Find tab of the Find and Replace dialog box matches the Replace tab except it lacks the replace function and only searches documents for items that you specify.

In the book, each skill is described in a two-page graphical spread (Figure 1). The left side of the two-page spread describes the skill, the concept, and the steps needed to perform the skill. The right side of the spread uses screen shots to show you how the screen should look at key stages.

Figure 1 (cont'd)

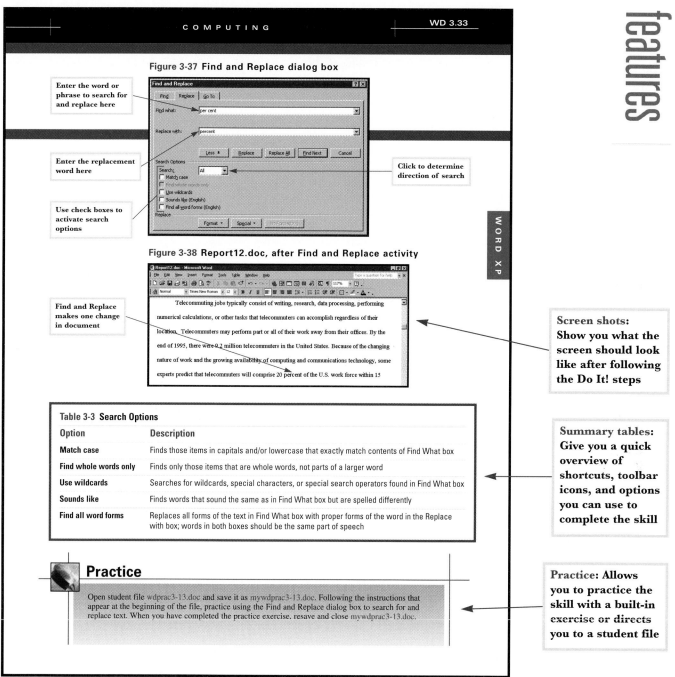

Figure 3-37 Find and Replace dialog box

Enter the word or phrase to search for and replace here

Enter the replacement word here

Use check boxes to activate search options

Click to determine direction of search

Figure 3-38 Report12.doc, after Find and Replace activity

Find and Replace makes one change in document

Telecommuting jobs typically consist of writing, research, data processing, performing numerical calculations, or other tasks that telecommuters can accomplish regardless of their location. Telecommuters may perform part or all of their work away from their offices. By the end of 1995, there were 9.2 million telecommuters in the United States. Because of the changing nature of work and the growing availability of computing and communications technology, some experts predict that telecommuters will comprise 20 percent of the U.S. work force within 15

Screen shots: Show you what the screen should look like after following the Do It! steps

Table 3-3 Search Options

Option	Description
Match case	Finds those items in capitals and/or lowercase that exactly match contents of Find What box
Find whole words only	Finds only those items that are whole words, not parts of a larger word
Use wildcards	Searches for wildcards, special characters, or special search operators found in Find What box
Sounds like	Finds words that sound the same as in Find What box but are spelled differently
Find all word forms	Replaces all forms of the text in Find What box with proper forms of the word in the Replace with box; words in both boxes should be the same part of speech

Summary tables: Give you a quick overview of shortcuts, toolbar icons, and options you can use to complete the skill

Practice

Open student file wdprac3-13.doc and save it as mywdprac3-13.doc. Following the instructions that appear at the beginning of the file, practice using the Find and Replace dialog box to search for and replace text. When you have completed the practice exercise, resave and close mywdprac3-13.doc.

Practice: Allows you to practice the skill with a built-in exercise or directs you to a student file

WORD XP

features

END-OF-LESSON FEATURES

In the book, the learning in each lesson is reinforced at the end by a Quiz and a skills review called Interactivity, which provides step-by-step exercises and real-world problems for the students to solve independently.

The following is a list of supplemental material available with the Interactive Computing Series:

Skills Assessment

SimNet eXPert (Simulated Network Assessment Product)—SimNet provides a way for you to test students' software skills in a simulated environment. SimNet is available for Microsoft Office 97, Microsoft Office 2000, and Microsoft Office XP. SimNet provides flexibility for you in your course by offering:

• Pre-testing options
• Post-testing options
• Course placement testing
• Diagnostic capabilities to reinforce skills
• Proficiency testing to measure skills
• Web or LAN delivery of tests
• Computer based training materials (New for Office XP)
• MOUS preparation exams
• Learning verification reports
• Spanish Version

Instructor's Resource Kits

The Instructor's Resource Kit provides professors with all of the ancillary material needed to teach a course. McGraw-Hill/Irwin is dedicated to providing instructors with the most effective instruction resources available. Many of these resources are available at our Information Technology Supersite www.mhhe.com/it. Our Instructor's Kits are available on CD-ROM and contain the following:

Diploma by Brownstone—is the most flexible, powerful, and easy-to-use computerized testing system available in higher education. The diploma system allows professors to create an Exam as a printed version, as a LAN-based Online version, and as an Internet version. Diploma includes grade book features, which automate the entire testing process.

Instructor's Manual—Includes:
–Solutions to all lessons and end-of-unit material
–Teaching Tips
–Teaching Strategies
–Additional exercises

PowerPoint Slides—NEW to the *Interactive Computing Series*, all of the figures from the application textbooks are available in PowerPoint slides for presentation purposes.

Student Data Files—To use the *Interactive Computing Series*, students must have Student Data Files to complete practice and test sessions. The instructor and students using this text in classes are granted the right to post the student files on any network or stand-alone computer, or to distribute the files on individual diskettes. The student files may be downloaded from our IT Supersite at www.mhhe.com/it.

Series Web Site—Available at www.mhhe.com/cit/apps/laudon.

Digital Solutions

Pageout—is our Course Web site Development Center. Pageout offers a Syllabus page, Web site address, Online Learning Center Content, online exercises and quizzes, gradebook, discussion board, an area for students to build their own Web pages, and all the features of Pageout Lite. For more information please visit the Pageout Web site at www.mhla.net/pageout.

Digital Solutions (continued)

OLC/Series Web Sites – Online Learning Centers (OLCs)/Series Sites are accessible through our Supersite at www.mhhe.com/it. Our Online Learning Centers/Series Sites provide pedagogical features and supplements for our titles online. Students can point and click their way to key terms, learning objectives, chapter overviews, PowerPoint slides, exercises, and Web links.

The McGraw-Hill Learning Architecture (MHLA) – is a complete course delivery system. MHLA gives professors ownership in the way digital content is presented to the class through online quizzing, student collaboration, course administration, and content management. For a walk-through of MHLA visit the MHLA Web site at www.mhla.net.

Packaging Options – For more about our discount options, contact your local McGraw-Hill/Irwin Sales representative at 1-800-338-3987 or visit our Web site at www.mhhe.com/it.

Visit www.mhhe.com/it
THE ONLY SITE WITH ALL YOUR CIT AND MIS NEEDS.

acknowledgments

The *Interactive Computing Series* is a cooperative effort of many individuals, each contributing to an overall team effort. The Interactive Computing team is composed of instructional designers, writers, multimedia designers, graphic artists, and programmers. Our goal is to provide you and your instructor with the most powerful and enjoyable learning environment using both traditional text and interactive techniques. Interactive Computing is tested rigorously prior to publication.

Our special thanks to George Werthman, our Publisher; Sarah Wood, our Developmental Editor; and Jeffrey Parr, Marketing Director for Computer Information Systems. They have provided exceptional market awareness and understanding, along with enthusiasm and support for the project, and have inspired us all to work closely together. In addition, Steven Schuetz provided valuable technical review of our interactive versions, and Charles Pelto contributed superb quality assurance.

The Azimuth team members who contributed to the *Interactive Computing Series* are:

Ken Rosenblatt (Editorial Director, Writer)
Russell Polo (Technical Director)
Robin Pickering (Developmental Editor, Writer)
David Langley (Writer)
Chris Hahnenberger (Multimedia Designer)

Interactive Computing Series

Microsoft® Access 2002 Brief Edition

contents

Access 2002 Brief Edition

⑤ Skill covers at least one MOUS Certification objective.

Access 2002 continued

Ⓢ Skill covers at least one MOUS Certification objective.

one

Introduction to Databases

A database is a collection of related information that is used to store, organize and extract data. Most, if not all, businesses today maintain one or more databases. For example, banks must have systems for keeping track of customers and their accounts, retail stores use point of sales systems to process the purchase of goods, and airlines use a database system for booking flights. Databases can be computerized as well as non-computerized. Some examples of non-computerized databases are telephone books, address books, and card catalogs in libraries. The advantage of a computerized database is the almost limitless capacity to store data, and the speed, accuracy, and efficiency with which you can retrieve information.

A computerized database built in Access is also flexible. Data can be reorganized and accessed in many different ways. In a computerized database, information is organized into tables. An Access database is a repository for these tables and the queries, forms, reports, and other database objects, which you will learn about in this book.

Relational databases enable you to link records from two or more tables based upon the data in a common field. The benefit is that you can save disk space and time because all of the fields in the database need not be filled in for each new entry. For example, a retail outlet would need an ordering system. For each order you would have to obtain the customer billing information, list each item the customer is purchasing and its cost, and subtract the items ordered from inventory. Instead of entering all of this information for each order, you would set up a Customer table to hold the customer billing information. Each customer will be assigned a unique customer number. An Inventory table will store details about the products the establishment stocks including the price/unit and the quantities in stock and on back order. Each product will be assigned a unique product number. Finally an Order table will store the information for each order placed with the company. The fields in the Order table will only have to include the Customer number, the Product number, and the quantity being ordered. The idea is that any piece of information is entered and stored only once, eliminating duplications of effort and the possibility of inconsistency between different records. Data entry errors are dramatically reduced because information only has to be entered once. As you continue through this book, these concepts will become clear to you. You will learn how to build a relational database with shared fields that link tables so that data redundancy is controlled and data inconsistency is avoided.

skills

- ⚡ **Opening an Existing Database**
- ⚡ **Navigating in Datasheet View**
- ⚡ **Working in Table Design View**
- ⚡ **Formatting a Datasheet**
- ⚡ **Creating a Drop-Down List**
- ⚡ **Entering Records in a Datasheet**
- ⚡ **Editing Records in a Datasheet**
- ⚡ **Understanding Shared Fields**
- ⚡ **Getting Help and Exiting Access**

Lesson Goal:

Become familiar with the structure of databases, the structure of tables, and the different data types that are used for the fields in a table. Learn how to navigate in a datasheet, add and edit records in a table, format a datasheet, and add a field to a table. Learn about the benefits of shared fields and how to get help while you work.

skill Opening an Existing Database

concept

There are several ways to start the Access program. You can use the Office Shortcut Bar if you have installed it, you can right-click the desktop, highlight New, and choose Microsoft Access on the shortcut menu, or you can use the Start menu. Using the Start menu will work on any computer no matter what settings or installation methods have been employed. After you start Access, you can choose to either start a new blank database or open an existing one.

do it !

Open an existing database and examine the application window.

1. Insert the disk containing your Access Student Files in the appropriate drive (if applicable). Click the Start button 🏁 Start on the Windows taskbar. Use the mouse to point to Programs. Click Microsoft Access on the Programs submenu to open Access.

2. Click the Open button 📂 on the Database toolbar, or click 📂 More files... on the New Task Pane on the right side of the application window to open the Open dialog box.

3. Click the list arrow on the Look in list box. Locate the disk drive where your Access Student Files are located. A list of the files and folders on the disk appears in the Contents window. If necessary, double-click the folder containing your Access Student Files.

4. Click Office Furniture Inc in the Contents window and click 📂 Open ▾ . The Office Furniture Inc database window opens.

5. Look at each of the Access window elements identified in Figure 1-1. The Objects bar on the left side of the Database window lists the seven types of database objects. Table 1-1 describes the objects.

6. Click Edit on the Menu bar. Point to the double arrows at the bottom of the menu to display all of the commands on the menu. Point to View on the Menu bar, then Insert, then Tools. Each menu opens in turn. Click the application title bar or anywhere in the application window to close the menu.

7. Place the mouse pointer over the buttons on the Database toolbar. Read the ScreenTips to begin to familiarize yourself with the program.

8. On the Database window toolbar, click the Large Icons button 🔲. The buttons on the Objects bar and the icons in the Database window change size.

9. Click the Queries button on the Objects bar. The commands for creating a query and the queries in the database are now displayed in the Database window.

10. Click Tables on the Objects bar. Click the List View button 🔲 on the Database window toolbar to return to the default view.

more

The application Title bar contains the application Control menu icon, the name of the application and the sizing buttons. The sizing buttons located in the upper-right corner of the Access title bar control how you view the application window. The Maximize button expands the window so that it fills the entire screen. The Minimize button reduces the application window to a program button on the Windows Taskbar. When the window is maximized, the Restore button replaces the Maximize button. Clicking the Restore button will revert the window to its previous size and location.

The Database window has its own title bar, Control menu icon, and sizing buttons. The Close button on the Database window Title bar will close the database but leave the Access program running. Both the task pane (under Open a file) and the bottom of the File menu list the last four databases you have opened. You can use these shortcuts to bypass the Open dialog box and quickly open a database on which you have recently worked.

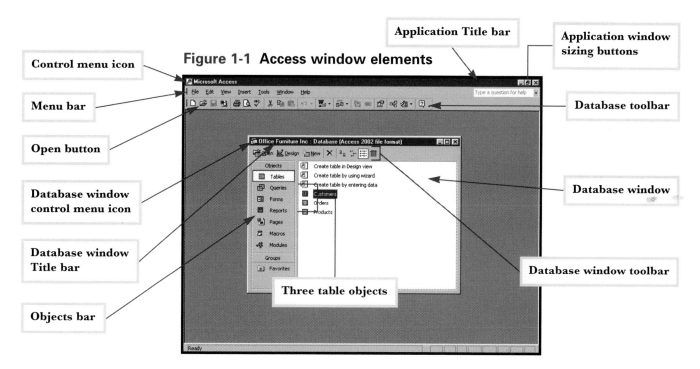

Figure 1-1 Access window elements

Application Title bar

Application window sizing buttons

Control menu icon

Menu bar

Open button

Database window control menu icon

Database window Title bar

Objects bar

Database toolbar

Database window

Database window toolbar

Three table objects

Table 1-1 Database Objects

Tables	The basis for the database. Tables are collections of records with similar data. You can link related tables to cut down on redundant or duplicated data and to make your data more manageable.
Queries	Allow you to select specific data from one or more tables. Queries enable you to create subsets of data by weeding out data you don't need at present. You use a query to clearly see and work with specific information
Forms	Data entry sheets that commonly contain the fields comprising a single record. The popular one record per screen format facilitates data entry and editing.
Reports	Used to present processed data in an organized format specifically designed for printing.
Pages	Data Access Pages (DAP). They are Web pages that allow you to view and work with data that is stored in an Access database on the Internet or a company intranet.
Macros	A series of keystrokes and commands that automate repetitive or complicated database tasks. You choose from a list of available actions and set them in a specific order to turn a multistep task into a one-click operation.
Modules	Functions and procedures written in the Visual Basic for Applications (VBA) programming language. In Access 2002 you use VBA to automate database tasks. VBA procedures can perform operations that exceed the capabilities of standard macros.

Practice

Use the Start menu to open a second Access application window. Locate and open the Home Video Collection database among your Access Student Files. Leave this application window open to complete the remaining Practice sections in this lesson. Minimize the window to return to the application window for the Office Furniture database.

skill

Navigating in Datasheet View

concept

All tables are structured in a specific way. Each piece of information is called a field. A set of related fields is called a record. Each record is entered across a row. You create column headings for each field. A record contains one field for each column heading. A column contains the fields for one particular kind of data. For example, phone numbers can be listed down in one of the columns. You view the fields in a table in Datasheet View.

do it !

Open the Customers table and learn to navigate in a table.

1. With the Office Furniture Inc database open and Tables selected on the Objects bar, click the Customers table icon in the Database window. Click [Open] on the Database window toolbar to open the table in Datasheet View. The Open button opens the selected object in its default view.

2. If necessary, click the Close button ⊠ on the Task Pane so that you can clearly see the Customers table.

3. There are 20 customer records organized into seven fields. The field names are listed at the top of each column. Each column heading is a field selector, which you can use to select the column. Click the Company Name field selector.

4. You can also select more than one column by dragging across the fields you wish to select. Click the Billing Address field selector and drag to the right to select the City and State columns.

5. Click the first field in the Customer ID column. The Specific Record box at the bottom of the datasheet window identifies the currently selected record. To the left of the first field column is a column of gray boxes called Record selectors. The Current record symbol ▶ in the Record selector box also indicates the active record.

6. Press [Tab] on the keyboard to move to the next field in the first record. Albert's Retail should be highlighted as shown in Figure 1-2. Press [Enter]. The third field is now selected. You can press either [Tab] or [Enter] to move the focus to the next field.

7. Double-click in the Specific Record box. Type: 13. Press [Enter]. The focus moves to record 13. Click the Next Record button ▶ (to the right of the Specific Record box). The focus moves to the next record on the datasheet.

8. Click the Last Record button ▶I. Press [Ctrl]+[Home] on the keyboard to return the focus to the first record on the datasheet.

9. The Record selector box in the row after the last record in the table contains the New record symbol ✳ (see Table 1-2). If you click the New record navigation button ▶✳ the focus will shift to this row and you can begin entering a new record.

10. Close the Customers table by clicking the Close button ⊠ on the table's Title bar.

more

You can also use the arrow keys on the keyboard to move between the fields in a datasheet. However, if you click a field with the mouse to select it, the program will shift to Edit mode. In Edit mode the left and right arrow keys will not switch the focus to the next field in a record. Instead, pressing the left and right arrow keys will move the insertion point within the text in the field. When you press [Tab] or [Enter] to move to the next field, the program will return to Navigation mode. You can also press the up (or down) arrow key to move to the same field in the next record (or previous record). This also returns the program to Navigation mode.

You can also use the keyboard combination [Ctrl] + [+] to move the focus to a new record. ◀▬▶ Open the Edit menu and highlight Go To to find another way to navigate within a datasheet. Commands corresponding to the navigation buttons at the bottom of the datasheet are located on the Go To submenu.

Figure 1-2 Navigating in a table

Current record symbol

Record selector

New record symbol

Click here to view the first record

Click here to view the previous record

Specific Record box

Click here to view the next record

Click here to view the last record

New record

Field names (Field selectors)

Total number of records

Access 2002

Table 1-2 Record Selectors

Button	Indicates
▶	Current record; the record has been saved as it appears
✳	A new record to which you can add data
✎	A record that is being edited and whose changes have not yet been saved
🔑▶	A record that is set as the primary key (in a table's Design View)

Practice

Click the second Microsoft® Access database button on the taskbar to maximize the window. Open the Home Video Collection table in Datasheet View. Select the Genre column. Drag to select the Title and Genre ID columns. Use the Specific record box to navigate to record 23. Use the [Tab] key to tab through the fields in record 23. Use the Next Record button to navigate to the last field in record 24. Close the Home Video Collection table and minimize the application window.

skill Working in Table Design View

MOUS Skill

concept

The smallest element of data is a field. When you are designing a table you should break your data down into as many fields as possible. This will give you the greatest flexibility in retrieving data later. For each field you create in a table you must specify a data type. The data type designates what kind of data the field can accept, for example, text, numbers, currency, or date and time data.

do it !

Open the Orders table and examine the data types assigned to the fields. Learn to work in the Design View window.

1. With the Office Furniture Inc database open and Tables selected on the Objects bar, click the Orders table in the Database window. Click ☑ Design on the Database window toolbar to open the table in Design View.

2. The Design View window is divided into two sections. In the top section you enter the field names, choose a data type for the field and enter a description of the field if necessary. The bottom half of the window is the Field Properties pane, in which you set other properties such as the field size, the number format, and the number of decimal places you want the field to include.

3. The fields in the Orders table include four different data types. Read Table 1-3 to learn about the main data types available in Access. The Order ID field is an AutoNumber field. This means that Access will automatically assign a unique number for each record in the order it is entered into the table.

4. Click in the Order Date field. Press [Tab]. Click the list arrow in the Data Type cell. Notice the different data types you can choose. Click the list arrow again to close the drop-down list. Make sure Date/Time is still the data type.

5. In the Field Properties pane in the lower portion of the window, click in the Format cell. Click the list arrow. The drop-down list displays the various Date/Time formats available in Access. Click Short Date to confirm the current choice and close the drop-down list.

6. To the left of the column of field names is a column of gray boxes called Row selectors. Click the Row selector next to the Product ID field to select the row.

7. Click the Product ID row selector again and drag upward until a black bold line appears underneath the Order ID row. Release the mouse to reposition the Product ID field directly under the Order ID field.

8. Click the Row selector for the Units Ordered field. Click the Insert Rows button ꔷ on the Table Design toolbar. Click in the Field Name cell of the new row.

9. Type: Ship Via, in the Field Name cell for the new row. Press [Tab]. Text is the default data type for a new field.

10. Double-click in the Field Size cell in the Field Properties pane. Type: 25 to set the field size property for the new field to 25 characters. The Design View window should now look like Figure 1-3.

11. Click the View button ▦ on the Table Design toolbar to return to Datasheet View. Click Yes to save the changes to the design of the table when prompted. Close the table.

more

Field properties are the attributes that describe and define a field. Only two properties are required, the field name and the data type. The data type determines the kind of data that can be entered into the field. You set other field properties in the Field Properties pane to further restrict the type of data that can be entered into the field. Setting field properties can also help you to reduce data entry errors. For example, you can reduce the field size for the State field in the Customers table to 2, so that only the two-character state abbreviation can be entered. If you accidentally begin a third character, the familiar Windows Ding will remind you that this operation is not allowed. You can also use a field selector in Datasheet View to change the position of a column in the table. First click the field selector to select the column. Then drag until a bold black line indicates the correct position for the column.

Table 1-3 Data types

Text	A text field can accept almost any characters you enter: letters, numbers, symbols, and most punctuation marks. You can assign a field size to limit the number of characters. The default size is 50 characters.
AutoNumber	An AutoNumber field automatically enters a sequential number as records are added to the table.
Number	Number fields can contain only positive or negative numbers. Usually you will assign this data type for fields that will be included in calculations in the database.
Currency	A currency field contains dollar amounts that will be displayed with dollar signs, commas, decimal points, and two digits following the decimal point. Currency fields can also be used in calculations.
Memo	Memo fields are used to hold large documents. You use a memo field when you want to store descriptive or narrative information. A memo field can hold up to 65,536 characters of text.
Date/Time	A date/time field holds date and time information in various formats. You must set a field in the date/time format in order to perform date calculations such as determining the number of days between two dates.
Logical Fields	A logical field accepts only Y/N (Yes/No) data. It displays in a table as a check box, a text box, or a combo box.
OLE object	Object Linking and Embedding object. Includes bitmapped graphics, drawings, waveform audio files, and any document prepared in another program.

Figure 1-3 Table Design View window

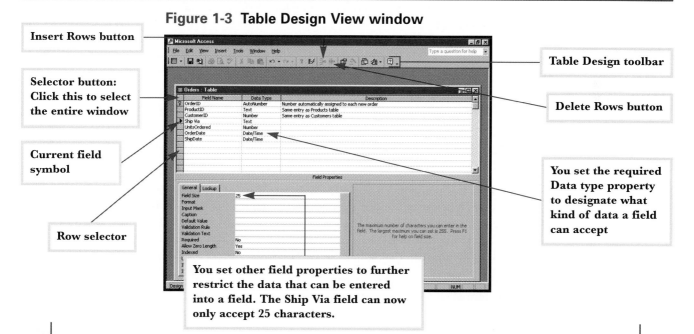

Insert Rows button

Selector button: Click this to select the entire window

Current field symbol

Row selector

Table Design toolbar

Delete Rows button

You set the required Data type property to designate what kind of data a field can accept

You set other field properties to further restrict the data that can be entered into a field. The Ship Via field can now only accept 25 characters.

Practice

Maximize the Access application window containing the Home Video Collection database. Open the Home Video Collection table in Design View. Use the Row selector to select the Comment field. Use the Insert Rows button on the Table Design toolbar to insert a new row. Name the new field Rating. Press the [Tab] key to automatically select the Text data type. Change the field size to 5. Save the changes to the design of the table and close the table. Minimize the application window.

skill Formatting a Datasheet

MOUS Skill

concept

Reports are the database objects that are specifically designed for printing, but you may want to print a table from time to time. You can enhance the appearance of a datasheet before you print it. Although you cannot change the appearance of individual cells, you can change the font, font style, and font color for the entire table. You can also change the background color, gridline color, and border or line styles for the table.

do it !

Format the Orders table.

1. Open the Orders table in the Office Furniture Inc database in Datasheet View. On the Formatting toolbar, click the list arrow on the Font box [Arial ▾]. Use the scroll bar on the drop-down list to locate the Times New Roman font and click to select it. If you do not see the Formatting toolbar, click View, point to the Toolbars command, and click Formatting on the Toolbars submenu to activate the toolbar.

2. Click the list arrow on the Font Size box [10 ▾] and change the font size to 12 pt.

3. Open the Format menu and click the Datasheet command to open the Datasheet Formatting dialog box. Click the list arrow on the first list box in the Border and Line Styles section at the bottom of the dialog box. Select Column Header Underline on the drop-down list.

4. Click the list arrow on the Gridline Color list box. Choose Maroon on the drop-down list. The settings in the dialog box are shown in Figure 1-4. Click [OK] to close the dialog box and apply the effects.

5. Click the list arrow on the Fill/Back Color button [▾]. Select the light green color (the fourth square) in the last row of the color palette.

6. Click the list arrow on the Font/Fore Color button [A▾]. Select the brown square in the first row of the color palette.

7. Position the mouse pointer over the right boundary of the Order ID field selector until it becomes a horizontal resizing pointer ↔. Double-click the right boundary to decrease the size of the column. Double-clicking the right boundary of the field selector will size a field to its "best fit." The best fit is the size that will accommodate the longest field entry in the column. In this case the column width will decrease to fit the field heading.

8. Click the Save button [💾] on the Table Datasheet toolbar to save the formatting changes. The formatted table is shown in Figure 1-5. Close the table.

more

You can also change the height of the rows in a table to provide more space for text or just to make the table look less packed with data. When you change the height of one row in a table, all of the rows in the table are affected. Position the mouse pointer on the border between two row selectors until the pointer becomes a vertical resizing pointer ↕. Drag up or down to increase or decrease the height of all of the rows in the table.

If you make formatting changes and forget to save them, Access will prompt you to save the changes to the layout of the table when you attempt to close it. You can also apply a Raised or Sunken special effect to the cells in a table. Use either the Special Effect button on the Formatting toolbar or choose the appropriate option button in the Cell Effect section in the Datasheet Formatting dialog box.

Figure 1-4 Datasheet Formatting dialog box

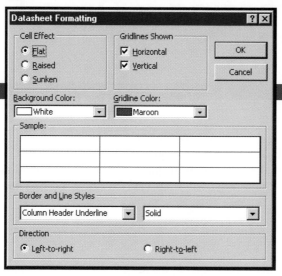

Figure 1-5 Formatted datasheet

Double-click the right boundary of a field selector to size the column to its "best fit," or drag the boundary to the left or right to custom size an individual column

Use the vertical resizing pointer to drag the border between any two row selectors to change the row height for the table

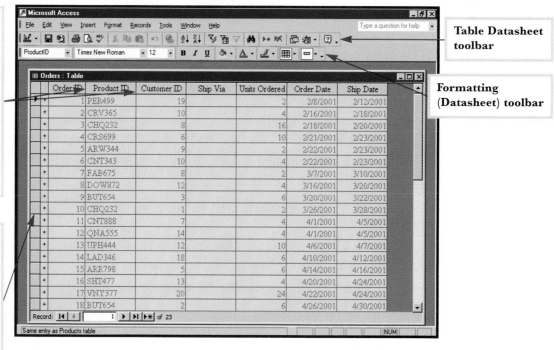

Table Datasheet toolbar

Formatting (Datasheet) toolbar

Practice

In the Home Video Collection database, open the Home Video Collection table in Datasheet View. Apply any design changes to the table that you wish including a new font, font size or style, font color, back color, and cell special effect. Change any column widths to their best fit as necessary. Change the height of the rows in the table. Save the changes, close the table, and minimize the window.

skill Creating a Drop-Down List

concept

You can use the Lookup Wizard to create a field with a drop-down list for a table. There are two kinds of Lookup fields you can create. A Lookup list displays values from an existing table or query. A Value list displays a fixed set of values that you determine when you create the field. Either way, data entry is made easier and data entry errors are reduced.

do it !

Make the Ship Via field in the Orders table a Value list.

1. Open the Orders table in the Office Furniture Inc database in Design View.

2. Click the Data Type field in the Ship Via row. Click the list arrow. Click Lookup Wizard in the drop-down list. The first Lookup Wizard dialog box opens.

3. Click the option button next to I will type in the values that I want. Click Next >.

4. Make sure the number of columns is set to 1. Position the insertion point in the field next to the current record symbol.

5. Type Federal Express. Press [Tab]. Type United Parcel Service. Press [Tab]. Type Airborne Express.

6. Double-click the right boundary of the column selector to resize the column to its best fit. The Lookup Wizard dialog box should look like Figure 1-6. Click Next >.

7. Make sure the label for the lookup column is Ship Via. Click Finish. The Ship Via field still has Text listed as its data type. Lookup fields are text fields.

8. Click the to save the change to the design of the table. Click the to switch to Datasheet View.

9. Click in the Ship Via field. A list arrow appears. Click the list arrow to view the new drop-down list.

10. Click the View button on the Table Datasheet toolbar to return to Design View.

11. Click the Lookup tab on the Field Properties pane. The properties for the lookup field are listed. You can see, as shown in Figure 1-7, that you have created a combo box with a Value list; the Row Source property lists the values you entered, and the Limit to List property is set to NO. This means that you can type in an alternative value that is not included in the Value list. That is the definition for a combo box; a text entry box in which the user has the option of entering text or selecting from a list.

12. Close the Design View window.

more

As you saw when you ran the Lookup Wizard, lists can contain more than one column. Additional columns can include descriptions of the list items. However, only one of the columns will contain the values for the drop-down list. The column that contains the data for the pick list is called a bound column. You will learn about bound and unbound columns as you continue through the lesson. You can change the Limit To list property on the Lookup tab to Yes to limit the user to only the values on the list.

Figure 1-6 Creating a Value List

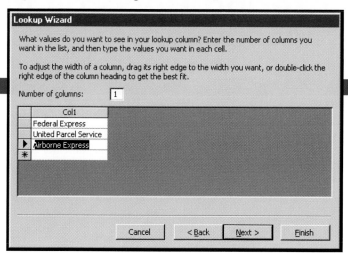

Figure 1-7 Lookup Field properties

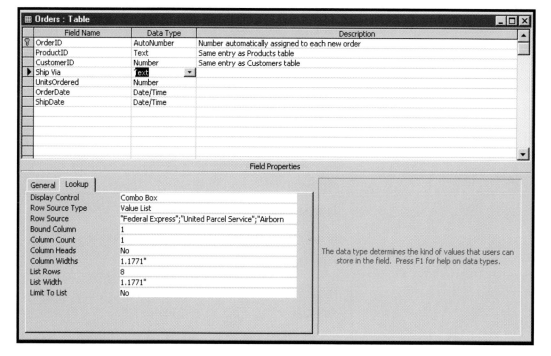

Practice

In the Home Video Collection database, open the Home Video Collection table in Design View. Click in the Data Type cell for the Rating field. Click the list arrow and choose Lookup Wizard on the drop-down list. Click the I will type in the values that I want option button. Click Next. Enter G, PG, PG-13, and R as the values for the drop-down list and complete the wizard. Click the Lookup tab to view the Lookup field properties for the Rating field. Save the changes to the design of the table, and switch to Datasheet View. View the drop-down list, close the table, and minimize the application window.

skill   Entering Records in a Datasheet

concept

As you will learn, data is usually entered into a database using a form. While forms are specifically designed to facilitate data entry, you can enter data directly into a table. A new record can only be entered at the end of a datasheet. When you enter data you do not have to worry about saving. Each time you begin a new record or switch to a different window the changes you have made to the records in the datasheet are saved.

do it !

Enter a new record in the Orders table.

1. With the Office Furniture Inc database open, double-click the Orders table in the Database window to open it in Datasheet View.

2. Click the New Record button ▶✳ on the Table Datasheet toolbar or the New Record navigation button ▶✳.

3. Press [Enter] to shift the focus to the second field in the record. The AutoNumber field will be automatically assigned. Type PER499. Press [Enter]. Type 5. Press [Enter]. Click the list arrow and select Federal Express. Press [Enter]. Type 8. Press [Enter]. Type 050801. Press [Enter]. Type 051001. Press [Enter].

4. Click the Maximize button on the Database window Title bar. Press the right arrow key on the keyboard [——▶] and enter the following record:

Product ID	DOW872
Customer ID	18
Ship Via	United Parcel Service
Units Ordered	12
Order Date	5/10/01
Ship Date	5/12/01

5. Increase the size of the Ship Via column so that entire entry can be viewed. Compare your updated Orders table with Figure 1-8.

6. Close the datasheet. You will be prompted to save the change to the layout of the table. The new record is automatically saved. ◗ With the Database window maximized, the Database window fills the Access application window and the sizing buttons for the Database window are on the Menu bar directly below the application sizing buttons.

7. Click the Restore button 🗗 on the right end of the Menu bar to restore the database window to its previous size and location.

more

How you enter data into a field depends on how the field was designed. The Customer ID and Units Ordered fields will only accept numbers. If you enter incorrect data a warning will display to inform you that the value you entered is not valid. Currency fields will also accept only numbers, which will be automatically formatted as currency. The combo box you created will accept either typed text or a selection from the list. You may have noticed that the date fields have already been formatted with the slash marks. This is called an input mask. Input masks are character strings that determine how data will display. Like properties, input masks limit the values a user can enter into a field. You will learn how to create an input mask in Lesson 2.

The two Control menus also contain commands for resizing and closing the Database window and the Access application window. The Control menu icon for the Database window is located to the left of the database name on the Database window Title bar. With the Database window maximized, it is on the left end of the Menu bar. The Control menu icon for the program is the key symbol just to the left of Microsoft Access in the program Title bar. The Control menus contain the Restore, Move, Size, Minimize, Maximize and Close commands.

Figure 1-8 Datasheet View with the Database window maximized

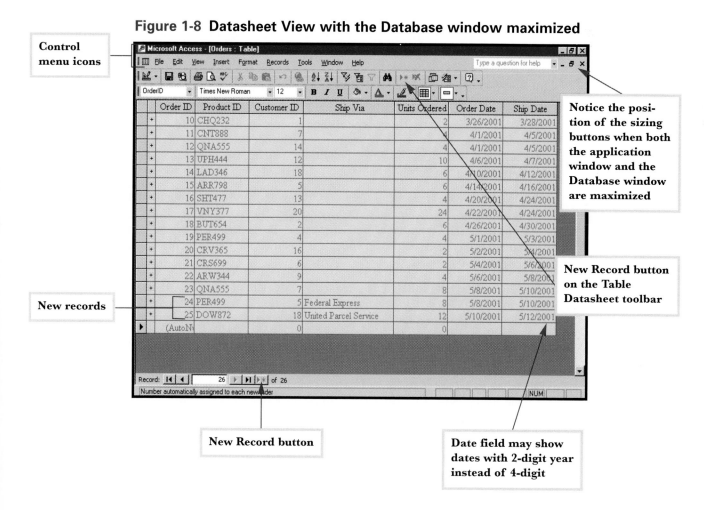

Control menu icons

Notice the position of the sizing buttons when both the application window and the Database window are maximized

New Record button on the Table Datasheet toolbar

New records

New Record button

Date field may show dates with 2-digit year instead of 4-digit

Access 2002

skill | Editing Records in a Datasheet

concept

In order to keep your database both accurate and current you will often have to edit certain records. You can change information you have entered in a field by selecting the text, positioning the insertion point, and using the Backspace and Delete keys on the keyboard. To make editing as efficient as possible you can also use a variety of other keystrokes and commands.

do it !

Edit records in the Customers table. Delete a record from the Products table for a product that the company is no longer going to carry.

1. With the Office Furniture Inc database open, double-click the Customers table icon in the Database window to open the table in Datasheet View.

2. Double-click in the Specific Record box near the bottom of the window. Type 15. Press [Enter]. Press [Tab] twice to move to the Billing Address field. Press [Delete]. Type 1667 Lansing Dr., to update the address. The Edit record symbol ⌀ displays in the Record selector while you are editing a record.

3. Click to the right of River in the Billing Address field for record 2 to position the insertion point. Type side, to make the street name Riverside. Use the right arrow key [→] on the keyboard to move the insertion point to the end of Road. Press the [Backspace] key three times. Type: d. to change to the abbreviation Rd as shown in Figure 1-9.

4. Press the down arrow key [▼] 4 times to move to the Billing Address field for record 6. Position the insertion point to the right of the letter e in Lindsey. Press [Backspace] and type a. Press [Tab] to move to the next field. Press [Esc]. The editing change you just completed is reversed. When you are still editing the same record you can use the [Esc] key to undo changes.

5. Click to the left of the r in Nartico in the City field of record 18. Press [Delete]. Type: n. Press [Tab]. Change the State entry to SC. Press [→]. Click the Undo button 🖙 on the Table Datasheet toolbar to reverse the changes you have made to the current record.

6. Click to the left of the n in Jonston in the Company Name field for record 15. Type h. Press [Tab] twice. Add Lake to the end of Indigo. Press [▲] twice.

7. In the City field for record 13, change Michaelton to Michaeltown. Press [Tab]. Change the state to NH. Press [▲]. Click Edit on the Menu bar. Click the Undo command. Notice that the command tells you that you are undoing the changes to the saved record. All of the changes you made to record 13 are reversed. Close the Customers table.

8. Open the Products table in Datasheet View. Select record 5. Click the Delete Record button 🖎 on the Table Datasheet toolbar to delete Product ID # CNT343. You will be prompted to confirm the deletion as shown in Figure 1-10, because it cannot be reversed. Click ⌗ Yes ⌗. Close the Products table.

more

In Edit mode you can either press [Esc] or click Undo to undo all of the changes you have made in the current record. However, after you have moved to another record and are back in Navigation mode, the changes are saved. You can no longer use the [Esc] key. You can, however, click Undo to reverse all changes to the last saved record. Press the keyboard combination [Shift]+[Tab] to return to the previous field. You can use the keyboard shortcut F2 to switch from Edit mode to Navigation mode. Use [Ctrl]+['] to insert the value in the same field in the previous record in the current field.

Figure 1-9 Editing Records

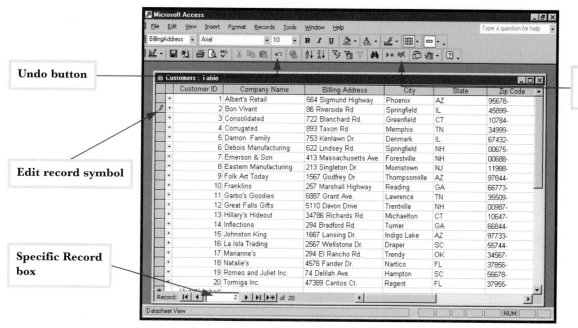

Undo button

Edit record symbol

Specific Record box

Delete Record button

Figure 1-10 Deletion warning dialog box

Practice

Open Microsoft Word using the Start menu. Then open the Word file acprac1-7.doc and follow the instructions it contains. When you have completed the exercise, close Word. You do not need to save any changes to the Word file.

skill | Understanding Shared Fields

concept

Each table in a database contains data about one subject. Each field, except the shared fields, should be stored in only one table. If a field in a table will cause the same piece of data to be repeated multiple times, it is in the wrong table. You want to be able to update information in only one place in the database and to avoid not only duplicate entries but entries for the same field that contain inconsistent data. Each table must also contain a unique field that identifies each record in the table. These are the shared fields that will allow you to connect data that is stored in separate tables.

do it !

Examine the relationships in the Office Furniture Inc database.

1. With the Office Furniture Inc. database open, double-click the Customers table to open it in Datasheet View. You may have noticed a column of plus signs ⊞, or expand indicators, in between the Record selectors and the first column of fields. This indicates that a sub-datasheet exists. A subdatasheet is simply a nested datasheet that contains related data. Click the expand indicator for the first record in the table. The shared Customer ID field links the record for Albert's Retail with the orders it has placed with Office Furniture Inc.

2. Click the expand indicator ⊞ to the left of the Order ID field in the Orders subdatasheet. The shared Product ID field links the Orders table with the Products table. You can now clearly see, as shown in Figure 1-11, that Albert's Retail placed an order on 3/26/01 for 2 channel quilted barstools. You can edit the data in the subdatasheets to change it in the joined table.

3. Click in the Ship Via field. Click the list arrow and choose Airborne Express on the drop-down list.

4. Click the Collapse indicators ⊟ to close the subdatasheets (or click the top indicator to close both subdatasheets at once). Close the Customers table and open the Orders table to view the updated record. Close the Orders table.

5. Click the Relationships button ⊞ on the Database toolbar to open the Relationships window as shown in Figure 1-12. Notice the line joining the Customers table and the Orders table. There is a 1 next to the Customer ID field in the Customers table and an infinity symbol ∞ next to the Customer ID field in the Orders table. This indicates that the value in the Customer ID field in the Customers table will match many records in the Orders table. The logical relationship has been established. One customer over time will place many different orders with a company. This is called a one-to-many relationship. You can see why the shared Customer ID field is so important. It allows you to build an ongoing customer purchase history with a minimum of effort. Each customer's purchasing history is automatically compiled as orders are entered in the Orders table.

6. Close the Relationships window. Open the Customers table in Datasheet View again. Understand that each customer number must be unique; that is, no two customers can be assigned the same number. Although at present the AutoNumber fields are listed in sequential order this will not always be the case. For example, if Customer ID #10, Franklins, were to go out of business, you might delete the record from the database. Customer ID #10 will never be reused.

7. Close the Customers table.

more Access automatically creates a subdatasheet for a table on the one side of a one-to-many relationship. You will learn more about relationships and how to create the relationships between tables in the next lesson. For now, you should understand that the design of a table is the set of instructions regarding the arrangement of the data within each record. These instructions include the type of data each field can accept and the format for that data, such as the number of characters allowed in each field. The unique identifier fields are used to logically link information in the database. In a rela-tional database you will tend to create many small tables because you can use the shared fields to establish relationships that will allow you to store information only once, organize it in a logical way, and bring it back together again in meaningful ways. A well-designed database should contain organized, related data that is stored only once. It should provide efficient data entry methods and include relationships that link basic entities.

Figure 1-11 Subdatasheets for the Customers table

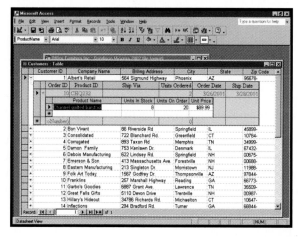

Figure 1-12 Relationships window

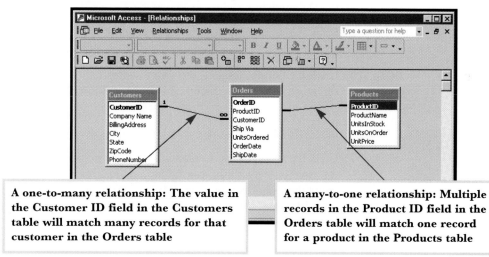

A one-to-many relationship: The value in the Customer ID field in the Customers table will match many records for that customer in the Orders table

A many-to-one relationship: Multiple records in the Product ID field in the Orders table will match one record for a product in the Products table

Practice

In the Home Video Collection database, open the Genre table in Datasheet View. Click the expand indicator for the first record in the table. The shared Genre ID field links the two tables. The movies that have been assigned the Genre ID # 1 for Sci/Fi Adventure display in the subdatasheet. Open several more subdatasheets to see the videos that have been placed in each genre category. Close the table and open the Relationships window. You can see the one-to-many relationship that has been created between the two tables. Each Genre ID # will be represented many times in the Home Video Collection table. Use the Close button on the application Title bar to close the Access application window containing the Home Video Collection database.

skill | Getting Help and Exiting Access

concept

There are a variety of ways to get help in Access. You can use the What's This command, ask the Office Assistant, or use the Ask a Question box on the right end of the Menu bar. The latter two features will generate a list of options. You click an option to open the Help window on that topic.

do it !

Learn how to use the Help facilities in Access.

1. With the Office Furniture Inc database open and Tables selected on the Objects bar, double-click the Products table icon in the Database window to open it in Datasheet View.

2. Click Help on the Menu bar. Click the What's This command. The mouse pointer changes to the What's This pointer ⬚?. Click the gray square at the top of the column of Record selectors at the intersection of the columns and rows in the table. A ScreenTip tells you that this is the Selector. You can use it to select the entire window to copy it to another program. Close the Products table.

3. Double-click in the Ask a Question box ⬚Type a question for help ⬚▾. Type field properties. Press [Enter]. The list of topics shown in Figure 1-13 opens. Click the first topic to open the Help window shown in Figure 1-14.

4. Click the second topic in the Help window to display text that will remind you how to change the Field Size property for a text or number field. Close the Help window.

5. Click the Office Assistant to open a search balloon. If the Office Assistant is not on the screen, open the Help menu and click the Show the Office Assistant command.

6. Type: editing a datasheet. Click ⬚Search⬚. A list of topics is added to the search balloon. Click the fourth topic, Troubleshoot editing data in a field in Datasheet or Form view.

7. Click the second topic to read why a value may not be allowed in a field. Some of the information may not be helpful at this time, but you should understand that entering a value that is not compatible with the data type for the field will cause Access to display an error message informing you that you cannot move to another field or record.

8. Click the Show button ⬚⬚ on the Help Window toolbar to expand the window to a two-paneled format (if you see the Hide button ⬚⬚ instead of the Show button, you are already viewing the two-paneled format). Click the Index tab at the top of the left panel. Position the insertion point in the Type keywords text box and type format. As you are typing, the list in the Or choose keywords list box scrolls to match the letters you type. ⬚⬚ When you are using the two-paneled Help window, the Show button becomes the Hide button. Click the Hide button to collapse the Help window back to the single-panel format (do not do this now).

9. Click ⬚Search⬚. All of the Help topics related to the keyword format display in the Choose a topic scrolling list box at the bottom of the window. (continued on AC 1.20)

Figure 1-13 List of Help topics

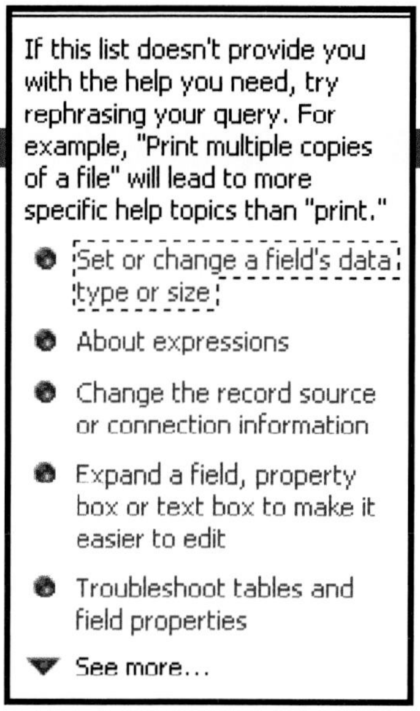

If this list doesn't provide you with the help you need, try rephrasing your query. For example, "Print multiple copies of a file" will lead to more specific help topics than "print."
Set or change a field's data type or size
About expressions
Change the record source or connection information
Expand a field, property box or text box to make it easier to edit
Troubleshoot tables and field properties
See more...

Figure 1-14 Microsoft Access Help window

Microsoft Access Help
Show All
Set or change a field's data type or size
If your table contains data, make a backup copy of the table before you change data types or field sizes.
Change a field's data type
Change the field size of a Text or Number field
Change the default field size of Text and Number fields

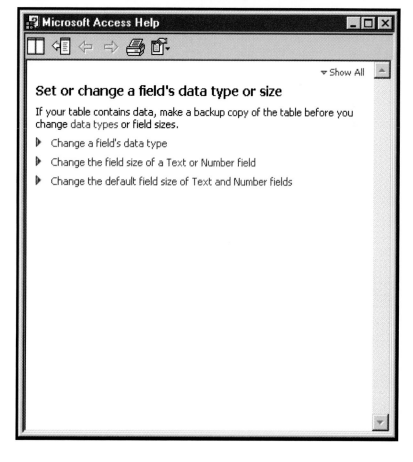

skill | Getting Help and Exiting Access (cont'd)

do it !

10. Click Format Property - Date/Time Data Type to display the Help window shown in Figure 1-15. Read about the pre-defined Format property settings for the Date/Time data type.

11. Close the Help window. Complete the Practice session.

12. Open the File menu and click the Close command to close the Office Furniture Inc. database. Open the File menu and click the Exit command to close Access. The Close command on the File menu corresponds to the Close button on the Database window title bar and thus will close the Database window. The Exit command corresponds to the Close button on the application title bar and thus will close the Access program.

more

The Contents tab contains every Help topic in Access broken down by category. A book icon represents each main category. Click the expand indicator next to one of the book icons to open the topic and reveal the subtopics. A page icon with a question mark on it designates each individual topic document. Click a document on the left to display it in the right half of the window. To close a Help category, click the collapse indicator next to the now open-book icon. Use the Back button on the Help window toolbar to return to topics you have previously viewed.

The Answer Wizard tab functions similarly to the Office Assistant. Enter a question in the What would you like to do? text box. Click the Search button to display a list of suggested topics in the Select topic to display box.

Figure 1-15 Help on Format Property feature

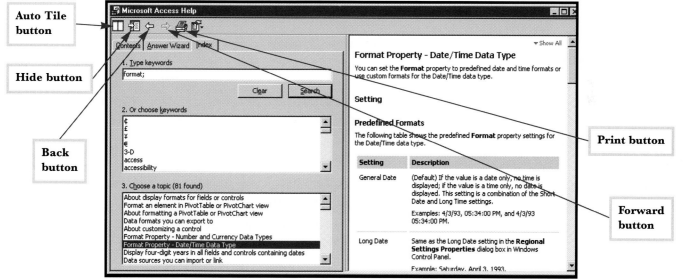

Auto Tile button

Hide button

Back button

Print button

Forward button

Practice

Type insert a field, in the Office Assistant search balloon and click [Search]. Open the Help window for the topic: Add a field to a table. Click Add a field to a table in Design View. Read the text to review some of the information you have learned in this lesson.

shortcuts

Function	Button/Mouse	Menu	Keyboard
Open a file		Click File, then click Open	[Ctrl]+[O]
Large Icons View in Database window		Click View, then click Large Icons	[Alt]+[G]
Small Icons View in Database window		Click View, then click Small Icons	[Alt]+[M]
List View in Database Window		Click View, then click List	[Alt]+[I]
Details View in Database window		Click View, then click Details	[Alt]+[D]
Switch to Datasheet View		In Table Design View, click View, then click Datasheet View	[Alt]+[V], [S]
Switch to Design View		In Table Datasheet View, click View, then click Design View	[Alt]+[V], [D]
Delete a row from a table		In Table Design View, click Edit, then click Delete Rows	[Alt]+[E], [R]
Insert a row in a table		In Table Design View, click Insert, then click Rows	[Alt]+[I], [R]
Begin entering a new record in a datasheet		Click Edit, point to Go To, then click New Record or click Insert, then click New Record	[Ctrl]+[+]
Delete a record from a datasheet		Click Edit, then click Delete Record	[Alt]+[E], [R]
Undo		Click Edit, then click Undo	[Esc] or [Alt]+[E], [U]
Fill/Back Color			
Font/Fore Color			
Open the Relationships window		Click Tools, then click Relationships	[Alt]+[T], [R]

A. Identify Key Features

Name the items indicated by callouts in Figure 1-16.

Figure 1-16 Microsoft Access window

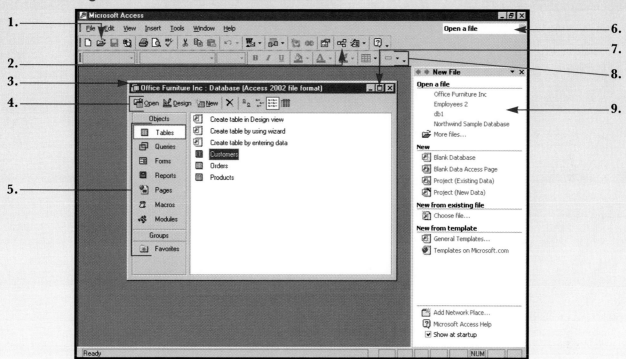

B. Select the Best Answer

10. A set of related fields is called a _____   **a.** Field

11. To the left of the first field column is a column of gray boxes called the   **b.** Field Properties

12. The basis for the database—collections of records with related data   **c.** Field selector

13. The Exit command on the File menu will close   **d.** Record

14. This designates what kind of data a field can accept   **e.** Database window

15. You set these to further restrict the type of data that can be entered into a field   **f.** AutoNumber

16. The smallest element of data is a _____   **g.** Tables

17. Data type that automatically enters a sequential number in the field as records are added to the table   **h.** Access

18. Each column heading is a _____ that you can use to select the column   **i.** Record selectors

19. The Close command on the File menu will close the _____   **j.** Data Type

quiz (continued)

C. Complete the Statement

20. A column contains:

a. Values of the same data type for different records

b. A set of related fields

c. A collection of different fields with related data

d. A collection of values in the same record

21. The set of instructions regarding the arrangement of the data within each record (the type of data each field can accept and the format for that data) is called:

a. The data type

b. The format property

c. The design of a table

d. The field properties

22. When you enter data in a table:

a. Only changes to the table design will be automatically saved, you must save new records frequently.

b. You must save frequently so that your data entry work will not be lost in the event of a power outage.

c. Each time you begin a new record or switch to a different window the changes you have made to the records in the datasheet are saved.

d. Access will remind you to save your data entry work when you close the table.

23. The two required field properties are:

a. The data type and the format

b. The field name and the data type

c. The field size and the format

d. The field name and the field size

24. The advantages of computerized databases over catalogs, index cards, and other paper methods are all of the following except:

a. The almost limitless capacity to store data

b. The speed, accuracy, and efficiency with which you can retrieve information

c. The highly organized method of storing data

d. The flexibility that enables you to reorganize and access data in many different ways

25. To navigate to the row in a table where you can begin entering the data for a new record, you can use all of the following except:

a. The keyboard combination [Ctrl]+[+]

b. The New Record navigation button

c. A field selector in Datasheet View

d. The New Record button on the Table Datasheet toolbar

26. A row contains:

a. All of the fields for one particular category of data

b. A set of related fields

c. A collection of different records with related data

d. A collection of related information

27. The advantages of a relational database are all of the following except:

a. Each piece of information must be entered and stored only once. You update data in one place and it is automatically updated throughout the database.

b. You can create links between tables to eliminate duplicate data and the possibility that the same item of data will be entered differently in two places.

c. Information is organized alphabetically for easy retrieval.

d. The number of data entry errors that can be made is dramatically reduced.

interactivity

Build Your Skills

1. Start Access and browse an existing database.

   a. Use the Start menu or any method you choose to start Access. Open the Recipes database in your Access Student Files folder.

   b. Open the Recipes table. Use the Specific Record box to navigate to record 48. Use the correct keyboard combination to return to the first record in the table.

   c. Use the correct navigation button to move the focus to the last field in the table.

   d. Press [↑] three times to move the focus to record 47. Press [Tab] three times.

   e. Press [Ctrl]+[End], the keyboard combination for moving the focus to the last field in the last record in the table.

2. Examine the Design View window, rearrange the fields, and insert a new field.

   a. Switch to Design View.

   b. Notice the Data Types used for each field. An OLE (object linking and embedding) object is simply a large object, usually a graphic but also any document prepared in another program. In the recipe database, the instructions for each recipe are (or will be when the database is complete) contained in an embedded Word document.

   c. Click in the TimetoPrepare field. Change the Field Size to 30.

   d. Use the Row selector to select the FoodCategoryID field. Move it underneath the RecipeID field.

   e. Select the TimetoPrepare field. Insert a new row. Click in the Field Name cell for the new row. Name the new field WhichMeal?

   f. Save the changes to the design of the table. Click Yes when warned about lost data. Return to Datasheet View.

3. Format a datasheet.

   a. With the Recipes table open in Datasheet View, maximize the window.

   b. Change the font for the table to Book Antiqua in a Bold style.

   c. Open the Datasheet Formatting dialog box and change the Gridline Color to Teal. Change the Cell Effect to Sunken. Close the dialog box.

   d. Change the Fill/Back Color to light yellow.

   e. Save the changes to the design of the table.

4. Create a drop-down list.

   a. Open the Recipes table in Design View. Click in the Data Type cell for the WhichMeal? field.

   b. Click the list arrow and select Lookup Wizard on the drop-down list.

interactivity (continued)

Build Your Skills (cont'd)

c. Click the I will type in the values that I want option button. Click Next.

d. Make sure 1 column is selected in the Number of columns text box. Type Breakfast in the first field. Press [Tab]. Enter Lunch, Dinner, Dessert and Appetizer as the other choices for the pick list. Size the column to the best fit. Click Next.

e. Make sure Which Meal? is selected as the label for the lookup column and click Finish.

f. Switch to Datasheet View. Save the change to the design of the table when prompted.

g. Click in the Which Meal? field of the first record, Hot Sausage Rolls. Click the list arrow and select Appetizer on the drop-down list.

5. Entering a record in a datasheet.

a. Click the New record button on the Table Datasheet toolbar.

b. Enter the following 2 records:

Recipe ID	Food Category ID	Recipe Name	Which Meal?	Time to Prepare	Number of Servings	Instructions	Vegetarian
Auto Number (Press[Tab])	1	Pepper Sirloin Steak	Dinner	25 min	6	(Skip)	No (leave unchecked)
Auto Number (Press[Tab])	10	Chocolate Turtle Cheesecake	Dessert	35 min	12	(Skip)	N/A (leave unchecked)

c. Right-click in the Instructions field for the Pepper Sirloin Steak record. Click Insert Object on the shortcut menu. Click the Create from file option button in the Microsoft Access dialog box. Click Browse to open the Browse dialog box. Use the Look in list box to locate your Access Student Files. Select the Pepper Sirloin Steak document and click OK. Click OK to close the Microsoft Access dialog box. The Instructions field now says Microsoft Word Document. Double-click in the field to view the embedded object.

d. Follow the instructions in the previous step to embed the Chocolate Turtle Cheesecake recipe in the Instructions field for the record.

6. Editing Records in a datasheet.

a. Change the Recipe Name field for Record 4 to Vegetable Chicken Pasta.

b. On record 11, change the number of servings to 6 and enter Dinner in the Which Meal? field.

c. On record 14, fix the spelling on Deviled and enter Appetizer in the Which Meal? field.

d. Change the Food Category ID on record 24 to 11. Enter Dessert in the Which Meal? field.

interactivity (continued)

Build Your Skills (cont'd)

7. Examine the relationship between the two tables.

    a. Close the Recipes table. Open the Food Category table in Datasheet View.

    b. Open the subdatasheet for the first record, Beef. The two recipes in this category display. Examine the other subdatasheets. The shared Food Category ID field links the two tables.

    c. Close the Food Category table. Open the Relationships window.

    d. A one-to-many relationship exists between the Food Category and Recipes tables. Each Food category will apply to many entries in the Recipes table.

    e. Close the Relationships window.

8. Get Help and exit Access

    a. Type designing a database, in the Ask a question box. Click About designing a database. Read the page.

    b. Click the Show button if necessary. Open the Contents tab. Click the expand indicator next to Microsoft Access Help.

    c. Click the Expand indicator next to Tables. Click the About Tables document.

    d. Click How data is organized in tables. Read the information and close the Help window

    e. Click the Close button on the application Title bar to exit Access.

Problem Solving Exercises

1. For each example of a database given below, write down at least five fields you would expect to find and examples of two possible records. Write down the data type for each field.

    a. CD collection

    b. Address book

    c. Book store inventory

    d. Coin collection

    e. Recipe file

    f. Teacher's grade book

    g. Sporting equipment catalog

2. You have been hired by Ruloff and Dewitt, a rapidly growing advertising agency that specializes in promoting new products and services. For your first project you must compile data on the magazine preferences of a cross-section of people. This data will eventually be stored and maintained in an Access database. Your initial assignment is to plan the database on paper following database design principles. First, make a list of the fields that should be included in the database. Create fields for the following:

interactivity (continued)

Problem Solving Exercises (cont'd)

a. a unique identification number for each record

b. First Name

c. Last Name

d. Age

e. Gender

f. Occupation

g. Number of Magazines Read Regularly

h. Favorite Magazine

i. Hobbies

Either collect or fabricate data for 25 people and write it down in a table format. Next, group the fields to form three different tables. Plan all three tables keeping in mind that you are planning a relational database. Make sure you write down the fields for each table and the data type for each field. Be sure to name all three tables. The three tables must share at least one common field (one of the unique identification fields) so that they can be joined later.

Creating Tables and Queries

Now that you are familiar with the Access application window, the basic structure of a database, and the structure and design of a table, you are ready to begin building your own databases. When you plan a database, you must first decide how many and what kind of tables your database will need. You will need to determine how the data you are collecting can be organized into separate smaller groups and how the fields in the tables can be related to each other. As you have learned, each table will contain fields related to one topic and each field will be assigned an appropriate data type to designate the kind of data that can be entered into the field. By focusing each table on a particular topic you simplify the structure of each table making them easier to modify later. As you have seen, the shared fields will enable you to link related information in other tables so that you can easily view all of the orders associated with a particular customer, all of the movies in a particular genre, or all of the recipes in a particular food category.

When you create a new database, you first create and save an empty database and then create the objects the database will contain. You can use a Database Wizard to quickly create a complete database on one of ten business topics. The simplest way to create a table is to use the Table Wizard. The Wizard guides you through a series of dialog boxes that help you to choose the fields for the database or the fields for the table. However, you will eventually want to create your tables in the Design View window to have more control over the finished product. As you have seen, in the Design View window you work with the underlying structure of the table. You enter the names for your fields and the data type for each field and set field properties for fields in which you want to alter the format or otherwise restrict the data that the field can accept. You must also identify the field that will serve as the primary key for the table. Primary keys are the fields containing the value that will uniquely identify each record in the table. In other words, the primary key is the shared field that will enable you to link the records in one table to records in other tables. When you have built all of the tables for your database you will create the relationships by forming joins between the shared fields.

After you have created your tables you can use various methods to reorganize data. You will learn how to sort data so that it is displayed in either ascending or descending order and filter data so that you can work with a temporary subset of records. You will also learn how to locate a specific piece of data using the Find command.

You create queries to answer questions about the data in your tables. These questions create permanent subsets of data. For example, you might want to know what customers have placed orders with your company in the last three months or what movies in your home video collection are rated PG. Queries allow you to focus on the data that you need to work with at present by eliminating all records in a table that do not match the criteria that you set.

Lesson Goal:

Create a database from a template. Create the tables to store the employee data for a company. Set and modify field properties. Learn to find, sort, and filter data and create queries.

skills

※ **Creating a Database with the Database Wizard**

※ **Using the Table Wizard**

※ **Modifying Field Properties**

※ **Creating an Input Mask**

※ **Setting a Validation Rule**

※ **Creating a Table in Design View**

※ **Establishing Table Relationships**

※ **Sorting and Finding Records**

※ **Filtering Records**

※ **Using the Simple Query Wizard**

※ **Creating a Calculated Field in a Query**

Access 2002

skill

Creating a Database with the Database Wizard

concept

The easiest way to create a new database is to use a Database Wizard. The Access Database Wizards provide a number of different databases that are commonly used in business. When you use a Wizard, all of the fields, tables, queries, forms, and reports that you will need in the database are created for you. You can examine one of the completed templates to give you a better idea of what all of the objects will look like and how to design your own custom database.

do it!

Create a database using a Database Wizard.

1. Start Access. Click General Templates in the New from template section on the Task Pane. The Templates dialog box opens. Click the Databases tab.

2. Select the Order Entry icon as shown in Figure 2-1. Click [OK].

3. The File New Database dialog box opens. Click the list arrow on the Save in list box and select the drive where your Access Student Files folder is located. Double-click the folder in the Contents window of the dialog box to place it in the Save in list box. Order Entry1 has been entered for you in the File name text box as shown in Figure 2-2. Click [Create]. Whenever you create a new database either with a wizard or from a blank file, you must first save it with the name you have chosen and in the location where you want to store it.

4. The Order Entry1 database is created and saved in your Access Student Files folder window and the Order Entry1 Database window opens. The first Database Wizard dialog box opens on top of it. Read the list of information the database will contain and click [Next >] to continue.

5. The next Wizard dialog box contains boxes that display the Tables in the database and the Fields in the table. You can scroll to the bottom of the fields in the Fields in the table list box to add the optional fields, E-mail address or Notes to the Customer information table.

6. Click each table name in the Tables in the database box and read the list of fields the table will contain. Click [Next >].

7. Click Sumi Painting to select it as the style for your screen displays and click [Next >].

8. Click Corporate, if necessary, to select it as the style for your reports. Click [Next >].

9. Keep the selected title for the database, Order Entry, and click [Finish].

10. The Database Wizard creates the database objects for the Order Entry database (this may take a minute or more). Then a dialog box opens telling you that you must enter your company information before you can use the database application. Click [OK].

(continued on AC 2.4)

Figure 2-1 Choosing a Database Wizard

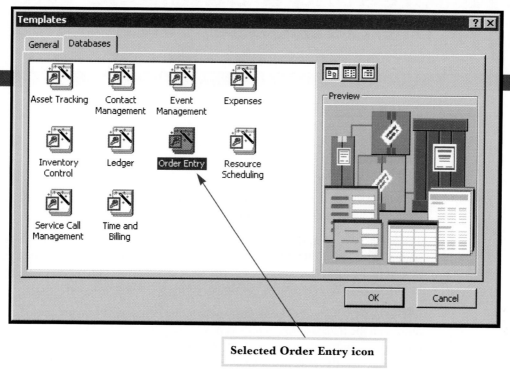

Selected Order Entry icon

Figure 2-2 File New Database dialog box

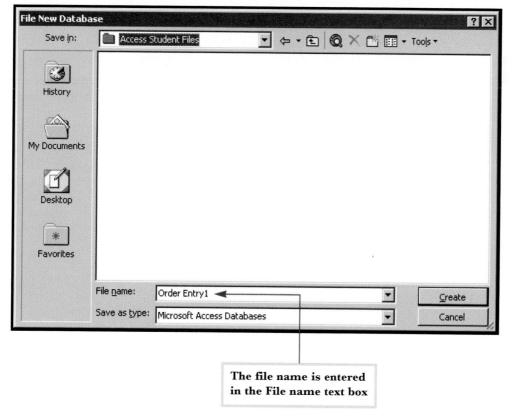

The file name is entered
in the File name text box

skill
Creating a Database with the Database Wizard (cont'd)

do it!

11. The My Company Information form opens. Enter the information given below into the form pressing the [Tab] key to move to each new field. Click the Close button on the form Title bar when you are finished.

    Browder's Comics, 6871 Franklin Dr., Ashlawn, MO, 84538, USA, .07, (skip the Default terms and Invoice description fields) 816-555-1766, 816-555-1767

12. The Main Switchboard opens as shown in Figure 2-3. Click Enter/View Other Information button ▣. Click Enter/View Employees button ▣. The Employees form opens as shown in Figure 2-4. You can see how a form will simplify data entry. Each employee record will be listed on a separate screen. Close the form. Close the switchboard.

    A switchboard is a custom window that contains command buttons for opening the objects in the database that a user is most likely to need. It will often contain buttons for opening the forms that data entry operators will use to enter information into the database. It will also usually enable management personnel to easily access the reports they will need to make strategic decisions.

13. Click the Restore button ▣ on the Order Entry title bar in the lower-left corner of the application window.

14. Click Tables on the Objects bar, then open the Employees table in Datasheet View, as shown in Figure 2-5. The Employees form you opened in Step 12 will be used to enter the Employee information into this table. Close the table.

15. Use the Objects bar to view the objects the Wizard has created for the database. Click Queries, then Forms, then Reports. Open several tables and their corresponding forms.

16. When you have finished close the Database window.

more

If a database contains a switchboard it usually opens first when the database is opened. All of the databases created with the Database Wizard include a switchboard. When you become more proficient with Access you can add a switchboard to the databases you create. You can use a switchboard to make it easier for new users to access the forms, reports or queries that they will need to use. You can also use a switchboard to control what objects in the database you will allow users to access.

Figure 2-3 Switchboard for an Access database

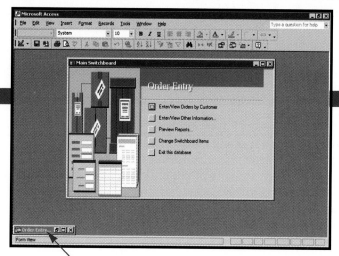

Order Entry Title bar

Figure 2-4 Employees form for the Order Entry database

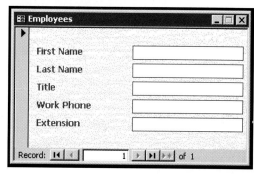

Figure 2-5 Employees table

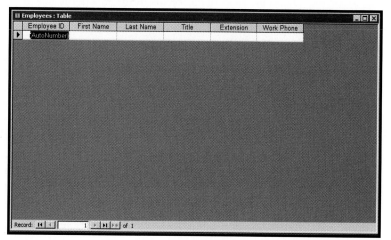

Practice

Click the New button 🗋 on the Database toolbar to reopen the task pane. Use the Database wizard to create the Expenses database. Apply any screen display style and Report style you choose. When the database is complete, use the switchboard to open and view the Expense eports by Employee form. Open several tables and their corresponding forms. Open the Relationships window and view the relationships between the tables. When you have finished, close the database. If storage space is a concern for you, you may delete this database.

skill | Using the Table Wizard

MOUS Skill

concept

After you have determined what tables your database will need and what fields you will need in your tables, you can begin to build your database. You can use the Table Wizard to easily build your first table. The Table Wizard provides a variety of pre-made business and personal tables. You can choose from among the fields offered in each type of table to create a table that fits your needs. The Table Wizard will choose the correct data types and field sizes for you and organize and assemble the fields in the table.

do it!

Create a new database file and use the Table Wizard to create a table.

1. Click the New button on the Database toolbar to re-open the Task Pane. Click Blank Database under New on the Task Pane. The File New Database dialog box opens.

2. Use the Save in list box to locate your Access Student Files folder. Double-click in the File name text box and type Employees 1. Click [Create]. The Employees 1 database is created and saved in your Access Student Files folder and the Database window for the Employees 1 database opens.

3. Double-click Create table by using wizard in the Employees 1 Database window. The first Table Wizard dialog box opens as shown in Figure 2-6.

4. With the Business option button selected as shown in Figure 2-6, click Employees in the Sample Tables scrolling list box.

5. Click Employee ID in the Sample Fields scrolling list box. Click the Add Field button [>] to add the field to the Fields in my new table box.

6. Double-click Last Name in the Sample Fields scrolling list box to add it the Fields in my new table box.

7. Use one of these two methods to add the First Name, Address, City, State or Province, and Postal Code fields to the Fields in my new table box. You will have to use the down scroll arrow on the Sample Fields scrolling list box to locate the fields. Click [Next >].

8. Keep the name for the table the Wizard has selected, Employees, and leave the Yes, set a primary key for me option button selected as shown in Figure 2-7. Click [Next >].

9. Click the Modify the table design option button as shown in Figure 2-8 and click [Finish]. The table opens in Design View. Notice the primary key symbol in the Row selector next to the Employee ID field. The Wizard has chosen the Employee ID field as the field you will use to link the records in the Employees table to records in other tables.

10. Leave the table open in Design View for the next skill.

more

The Table Wizard will automatically assign the Number data type and an appropriate field size to fields that will require only numbers. Fields for costs or prices will be assigned the Currency data type and fields such as the Required by Date and Promised by Date in the list of fields for the Orders table will be correctly assigned the Date/Time data type. When you use the Table Wizard to create a table you can choose fields from different sample tables, click Rename Field button [Rename Field...] to change a field name, and open the table in Design View to further modify the structure.

Figure 2-6 First Table Wizard dialog box

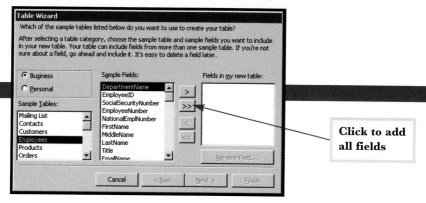

Figure 2-7 Second Table Wizard dialog box

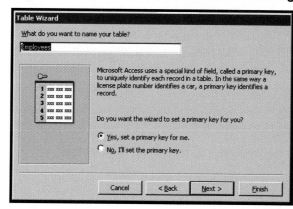

Figure 2-8 Final Table Wizard dialog box

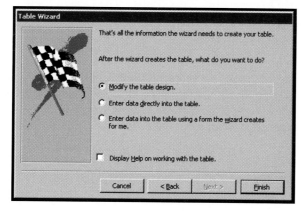

Practice

Use the Start menu to open a second Access application window. Open the Tuning Tracker database available in your Access Student Files folder. Use the Table wizard to create an Orders table. Select the Order ID, Customer ID, Order Date, RequiredbyDate, and PromisedbyDate fields. Let Access select the primary key for you and leave the name for the table, Orders. When you get to the third Wizard dialog box, simply click Next > . You will create the table relationships later in the lesson. Leave the Enter data directly into the table option button selected and click Finish. Resize the fields to display the complete column headings and save the changes. Close the table and minimize the application window.

skill   Modifying Field Properties

concept

You can use the Table Wizard to quickly create a table and then modify its properties in the Design View window to meet your needs. For example, you can modify the field names, set additional field properties, add field descriptions, or add fields that the Wizard does not offer.

do it!

Change field names, add field descriptions, add a field, and change field properties for the Employees table.

1. Click in the StateOrProvince field. Use [Backspace] and [Delete] keys to delete OrProvince. Double-click in the Field Size cell in the Field Properties pane and type 2, to restrict the field size. Press [Tab] to move to the Format cell.

2. Type >. The greater than symbol instructs Access to make all characters in the field upper-case. Each two-letter state abbreviation will be automatically capitalized. Press [Tab] twice to move to the Caption cell.

3. Change the Caption property for the field to State. Press [Tab].

4. Type NY, in the Default Value cell. For a company located in New York, this would be the most likely entry for the field. Setting a default value will save data entry personnel time when entering records.

5. Click in the Description cell for the State field. Type Default is NY; 2 characters limit; converted to uppercase. Press [Enter]. The Design View window should look like Figure 2-9. ◀▬▬ The description will display in the Status bar in the lower-left corner of the Access application window when the field is selected in Datasheet View.

6. Click in the PostalCode field. Change the field name to ZipCode. Press [Tab] twice and enter the description 10 character limit. Click in the Caption cell in the Field Properties pane. Change the Caption property to Zip Code. ◀▬▬ The Caption property controls the text that displays in the Field selector in Datasheet View. When a Caption property has been assigned, changing the Field Name property will not change the column heading.

7. Change the field size for the Zip Code field to 10.

8. Click the Row selector for the LastName field. Click the Insert Rows button ⬛ on the Table Design toolbar to insert a new row. Name the new field DateHired. Press [Tab].

9. Click the list arrow in the Data Type cell. Select Date/Time on the drop-down list. Press [Tab]. Type: Acceptable formats are 6/13/01, Jun 13, 01, or June 13, 2001.

10. Click in the Format cell in the Field Properties pane. Click the list arrow and select Short Date on the drop-down list. Data entry operators can enter any of the valid formats listed in the description, but all will be converted to the short date format, 6/13/01. This ensures that all data in the table will be displayed in a consistent format.

11. Enter Date Hired as the Caption property for the field. Check Figure 2-10 to make sure you have entered all of the properties correctly.

12. Click ⬛ on the Table Design toolbar to save the changes to the design of the table.

more It is considered good database programming practice not to include spaces in field names. Database programmers use an underscore to create spaces in their field names. This is because in programming languages object names cannot contain spaces. If a database programmer must write code for the field, they will have to change the field name. Tables that you create with the Table Wizard will follow this convention. The Caption property is used to create the conventional heading, with spaces, for the field. If you do not enter a Caption property, the field name will be used for the column heading.

Figure 2-9 Field Properties for the State field

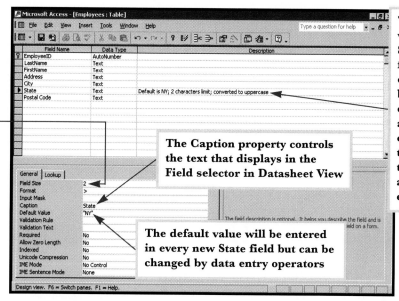

The greater than symbol instructs the program to capitalize the entries in the field

The Caption property controls the text that displays in the Field selector in Datasheet View

The default value will be entered in every new State field but can be changed by data entry operators

The field description will display in the Status bar when the field is selected. It explains that NY will be automatically entered into the field and that the field will only accept 2 characters, and the characters entered will be automatically converted to uppercase

Figure 2-10 Field Properties for the Zip Code field

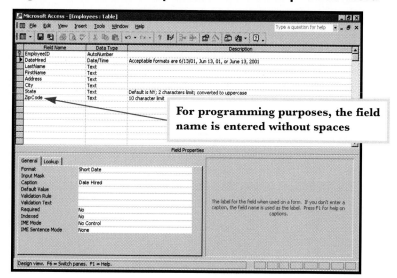

For programming purposes, the field name is entered without spaces

Access 2002

Practice

Open the Customers table in the Tuning Tracker database in Design View. Set the Format property for the State field so that all entries will appear as uppercase letters. Enter a description for the State field. Change the Field Size property for the City field to 25. Change the Field Size property for the Zip field to 10. Create a new field at the end of the table for PhoneNumber and enter the Caption property for the field. Save the changes. Click Yes if you receive a warning about changing a field size, no entry in the City field is over 25 characters so no data will be lost. Minimize the application window.

skill Creating an Input Mask

concept

Input masks are character strings that determine how data will display in a field. You can use the Input Mask Wizard to set the Input Mask property. The Input Mask property, just like all properties, is used to restrict the data a user can enter into a field. An input mask consists of literal characters (spaces, parentheses, dots, etc.), and placeholder characters. Placeholder text consists of characters such as underscores, which indicate to the user where the values for the field should be entered.

do it!

Use the Input Mask Wizard to set the Input Mask property for the Zip Code field.

1. With the Employees table in the Employees 1 database open in Design View, click in the Zip Code field. Click in the Input Mask cell in the Field Properties pane.

2. Click the Build button ... to the right of the Input Mask cell. The Input Mask Wizard opens.

3. Click Zip Code in the Input Mask/Data Look box. Use the scroll bar to view the various pre-defined input masks available in Access. Click Next > .

4. Click the list arrow on the Placeholder character list box and select # on the drop-down list.

5. Click in the Try It box. Navigate to the first placeholder character if necessary, and type 223076677. Each placeholder character is replaced as you type a literal character. The field is automatically formatted with the hyphen after the main 5 numbers in the zip code as shown in Figure 2-11. Click Next > .

6. Click the With the symbols in the mask, like this option button to display the hyphen in the data in the table. Click Next > . Click Finish . Press [Enter].

7. The completed Input Mask property is shown in Figure 2-12. The 0's for the first five digits of the zip code indicate that an entry is required for each placeholder. The 9's for the last four digits of the zip code indicate that these digits are optional. The slash before the (-) indicates that the hyphen is a literal character that will display in the field.

8. Click 🖫 to save the change to the design of the table. Click ▦▾ to switch to Datasheet View.

9. Scroll to the right and click in the first Zip Code field in front of the first character of the input mask. The input mask appears. Type 2230. Press [Enter]. A Microsoft warning dialog box opens because the first five required digits have not been entered. Click OK . Type 7. Press [Enter]. The zip code is entered in the field with the hyphen as the final character. The last four digits are optional. Close the table.

more

The Input Mask Wizard can only be used for Text or Date/Time fields. If you want to create an input mask for a Number or Currency field you must enter the formatting symbols yourself to create a custom input mask in the Input Mask property field.

Telephone numbers and zip codes should be assigned the Text data type even though they generally contain numbers. This is because you may want to enter a phone number containing letters and because when sorting fields with the Number data type Access will interpret a telephone number or zip code as a value. If you have entered the zip code 22307 in one place and the zip code 22307-7766 in another, and you sort a table to group records with like zip codes, 22307 will be interpreted as 22,307 and 22307-7766 will be interpreted as 223,077,766. The two zip codes in the same area of the country will not be grouped together in the table. 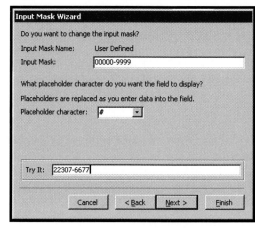 You use an input mask to control not only how data will display as the Format property does, but also how data is entered into a field and stored in the database. The input mask forces the user to enter data in the format that you have set.

Figure 2-11 Using the Input Mask Wizard

Figure 2-12 Input Mask property

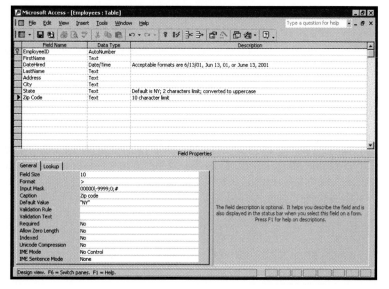

Practice

In the Customers table in the Tuning Tracker database, use the Input Mask Wizard to set the Input Mask property for both the Zip Code field and the Phone Number field. Use any placeholder characters you choose and store the data with the symbols in the mask. Save the changes after you create each mask. Switch to Datasheet View and increase the size of the Zip Code field to accommodate the zip code extensions. Save the change, close the table and minimize the application window.

skill Setting a Validation Rule

concept

One more method for restricting the values that users can enter into a field is to set the Validation Rule property for a field. A validation rule is a short expression that will test the reasonableness of an entry. If the value the user enters does not satisfy the validation rule criteria, an error message will display. You can set the Validation Text property to designate specific text for the error message. Validation rules allow you to precisely control the data that a field can accept and are yet another method of ensuring that your database contains accurate information.

do it!

Add a field for Gender to the Employees table. Set the Validation Rule property so that only the letters M or F will be accepted in the field. Set the Validation Text property to display a custom error message.

1. Open the Employees table in the Employees 1 database in Design View. Click in the first empty cell below the ZipCode field.

2. Type Gender. Press [Enter]. Leave the default, Text, as the data type.

3. Double-click in the Field Size cell in the Field Properties pane. Type 1. Press [Enter] to move to the Format property.

4. Type >, to program Access to capitalize all entries in the field. Press [Enter] four times to move to the Validation Rule property.

5. Type = M or F to set the validation rule. Access will test the data entered in the field to see if it passes the test. If the user does not enter an m or an f an error message will display. Press [Enter]. Quotation marks are inserted around the two acceptable characters.

6. Type You may only enter M or F to set the validation text. This message will display in the error dialog box if a user enters invalid data. The properties for the new field are shown in Figure 2-13.

7. Click 🖫 on the Table Design toolbar to save the change to the design of the table. The dialog box shown in Figure 2-14 opens. When you add a validation rule you must test the existing data to make sure that it conforms to the new rule. Since this is a new field and no data has yet been entered, click No .

8. Click 🖩▾ to switch to Datasheet View. Scroll to the right and click in the Gender field for the first record. Type W. Press [Enter]. The warning dialog box shown in Figure 2-15 opens with the text you supplied in the Validation Text property.

9. Click OK . Delete the w and type m. Press [Enter]. The entry is automatically capitalized as designated by the Format property. Close the table.

more

Validation rules such as the one created in the exercise, which are based on only one field, are called field-level validation rules. A more complex type of validation rule in which the value of a field depends on an entry that has already been made in another field in the current record is called a table-level validation rule. Data validation rules use expressions that result in one of two values, either True or False. If the result of the expression is True, the data is entered in the field. If the result is False, the error message you entered as the validation text will display.

Figure 2-13 Setting a Validation Rule

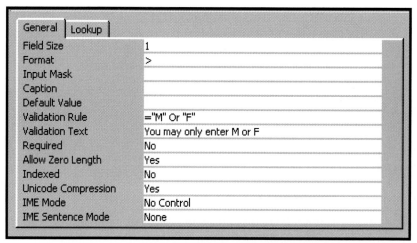

Figure 2-14 Warning dialog box that displays when a validation rule is added to a table

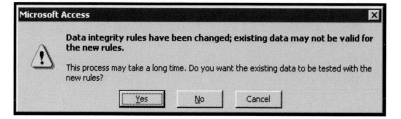

Figure 2-15 Warning dialog box containing the Validation Text

Practice

Open the Service Records table in the Tuning Tracker database in Design View. Change the Field Size property for the Use field to Byte. The Byte field size is the most efficient way to store numeric data that will not be greater than 255. Create a data validation rule to limit the entries in the field to 1–5. The expression is: >0 And <6. Save the change and click Yes to test the existing data. Enter the validation text: Only numbers between 1 and 5 are allowed. Save the change, switch to Datasheet View, and change the data in a record's Use field to test the new properties. Close the table and minimize the application window.

skill

Creating a Table in Design View

concept

Although a table created with the Table Wizard can be modified to fit your data, you will want to create tables on your own in order to have complete control over the field names, data types, and field properties. As you have learned, first you must identify the type of information your table will contain and then determine what data entities to include. Each data entity will be assigned to a field in the table.

do it!

Use all of the skills you have learned thus far to create a table in the Design View window called Positions for the Employees 1 database.

1. With Tables selected on the Objects bar on the Employees 1 Database window, double-click Create table in Design View. The Design View window for Table 1 opens.

2. Type EmployeeID in the first Field Name cell. Press [Enter]. Click the list arrow and select Number on the drop-down list. Press [Tab] two times.

3. Type Department. Press [Enter]. Set the Field Size property to 25.

4. Create a Text field for Title. Create a Currency field for HourlyRate.

5. Create a Yes/No field for StockOptionPlan. Click the Lookup tab. If Check Box is not already entered in the Display Control property, click the list arrow and select it from the drop-down list.

6. Create a field called Status. Use the Lookup Wizard to create a drop-down value list for the field. Enter Temporary, Part-Time, and Full-Time as the values for the pick list. Open the Lookup tab on the Field Properties pane as shown in Figure 2-16.

7. Create a Yes/No field for HealthPlan. Set the Default Value property for the field to Yes. (Type Yes, in the Default Value property cell.) On the Lookup tab, set the Display Control property to Check Box if necessary. The properties of the field are shown in Figure 2-17.

8. Set Caption properties for each field that you want to display in the column heading with spaces included.

9. Click the Row selector for the EmployeeID field. Click the Primary Key button [🔑] on the Table Design toolbar. The key symbol is inserted in the Row selector for the EmployeeID field as shown in Figure 2-17. ◀━━ Remember the primary key field is used to uniquely identify each record in the table. It will be used to link the employee records in the Positions table with the employee records in the Employees table.

10. Click [💾] on the Table Design toolbar. The Save As dialog box shown in Figure 2-18 opens. Type: Positions in the Table Name text box. Click [OK]. The table is saved in the Employees 1 database and the table name, Positions, displays in the Design View window title bar.

11. Click [▦▾] to switch to Datasheet View. Adjust the column widths to display the complete column headings. Notice that the Health Plan check box is checked because you set the default value for the field to Yes.

12. Save the changes and close the table. Notice that the new table, Positions, is listed under the Employees table in the Database window. Close the Employees 1 database.

more   A Yes/No field can appear as a check box, as a text box that displays Yes or No, or as a combo box that has Yes and No on a drop-down list. As you saw in the exercise, you set the Display Control property on the Lookup tab to choose the format you want. If you use a text box, data entry operators will enter -1 and it will be converted to Yes. 0 will be converted to No.

There are three kinds of primary keys. You can create the fields you need in a table without creating a unique identifier field. When you save the table, Access will ask if you want to have the program create a primary key for you. If you click Yes, an AutoNumber primary key field will be automatically created for you. In the exercise above, you created a single-field primary key. You used the Employee ID field which will have a unique value for each employee. If you need data from more than one column in order to meet the uniqueness requirement, you can designate two or more fields as the primary key. This is called a multiple-field or composite primary key.

Figure 2-16 Properties for the Lookup Field

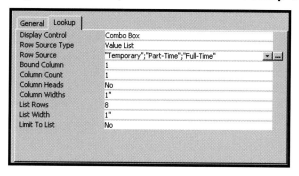

Figure 2-17 Design View Window for the Positions Table

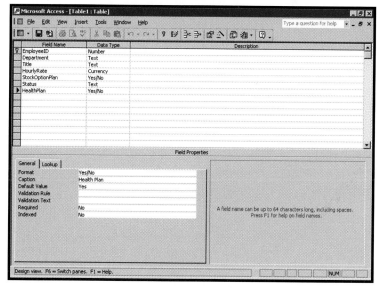

Figure 2-18 Saving a Table

Practice

Create a new table in Design View in the Tuning Tracker database. Name the new table Service History. Create a Number field for CustomerID, a Date/Time field for the TuningDates, and a Yes/No field for TuningDue. Apply the Short Date format to the TuningDates field. Set the Display Control property for the TuningDue field to check box. Set the Caption properties as necessary. Save the table and do not set a primary key. Close the table and minimize the application window.

skill Establishing Table Relationships

concept

After you have established a way of relating two tables with a common field, you can use the Relationships window to define the type of relationship and establish the joins. There are three types of relationships. You have already viewed a one-to-many relationship in which each record in one table is matched to one or more records in another table. In a one-to-one relationship, each record in one table is matched to only one record in the second table. In a many-to-many relationship, each record in one table is matched to many records in a second table and vice versa.

do it!

Open the Employees 2 database and establish table relationships.

1. Click ⬚ on the Database toolbar to re-open the Task Pane. Click 📂 More files... to access the Open dialog box. Use the Look in list box to locate the drive or folder where your Access Student Files are located. Double-click the folder to place it in the Look in list box. Double-click Employees 2 to open the database.

2. The Employees 2 database contains the Employees table that you built with the Table Wizard, a Position table similar to table that you built in the Design View window, and a third table in which the hours worked by each employee are recorded each week. Records for 51 employees have been added to all three tables.

3. Click the Relationships button ⬚ on the Database toolbar. The Show Table dialog box opens on top of the Relationships window. ⬛ If the Show Table dialog box does not open, click the Show Table command ⬚ Show Table... on the Relationships menu.

4. Press [Shift] and click the two un-highlighted tables in the Show Table dialog box to select all three tables as shown in Figure 2-19. Click ⬚ Add ⬚. The field lists for all three tables are added to the Relationships window.

5. Close the Show Table dialog box. Click the Employee ID field in the Employees table field list. Drag the selected field name toward the Employee ID field in the Hours table. As you drag, a small rectangle will display. Do not release the mouse button until the rectangle is over the Employee ID field in the Hours table's field list. The Edit Relationships dialog box opens as shown in Figure 2-20. Access has determined that you are creating a one-to-many relationship as shown at the bottom of the dialog box. Each employee will have one record in the Employees table and a record for the hours worked every week in the Hours table. ⬛ The primary key field for a table will be bold in the field list. To display all of the field names on a field list, Drag the bottom border to increase its size.

6. Select the Enforce Referential Integrity check box (see Figure 2-20). Referential integrity helps reduce data entry errors by ensuring that information in the two related fields matches. You cannot enter data in the field on the Many side of a relationship that does not exist in the related field on the One side.

(continued on AC 2.18)

Figure 2-19 Show Table dialog box

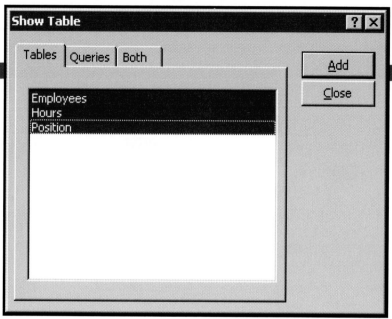

Figure 2-20 Edit Relationships dialog box

Select to
enforce
referential
integrity

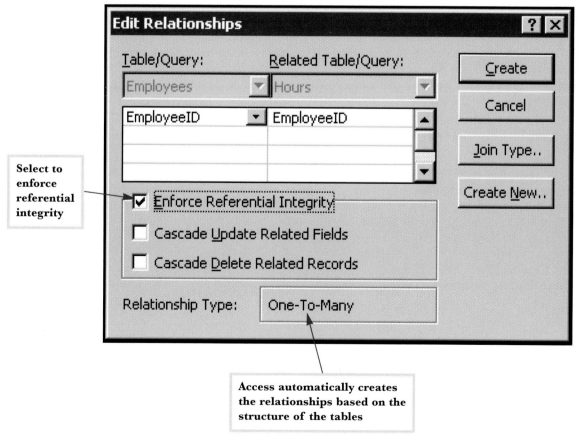

Access automatically creates
the relationships based on the
structure of the tables

skill Establishing Table Relationships (cont'd)

do it!

7. Click [Create]. The join is created and a line appears between the two fields to indicate that they are related. The infinity sign [∞] indicates the many side of the relationship.

   ▬ If you do not enforce referential integrity, the joins will be created but the 1 and the infinity symbol will not appear on the line between the joined fields.

8. Select the Employee ID field in the Employees table field list again. Click and drag the field to the Employee ID field in the Position table field list. The Edit relationships dialog box again opens. This time Access has correctly interpreted that you are creating a one-to-one relationship as shown at the bottom of the dialog box and in Figure 2-21.

9. Enforce referential integrity and click [Create].

10. Move the Position field list by clicking and dragging the title bar so that you can clearly see the relationships and your window looks like Figure 2-22.

11. Close the Relationships window. Click [Yes] to save the changes to the layout of the window.

more

When you create relationships, the related fields must have the same data type. However an AutoNumber primary key field can be linked to a Number field as long as the Field Size property for both fields is set to Long Integer. Long Integer is the default field size for a number field. Two Number fields must also have the Long Integer field size in order to establish a link. You set the Field Size property for a Number field to raise or lower the storage requirement for the field. The Byte field size has the lowest storage requirement (takes up the least space in the memory of the computer). You can use it for fields that will only need to hold entries between 0 and 255. The Integer field size is the next most efficient data type. You can use it to store entries between $-32,768$ and $+32,768$. Long Integers can be between $-2,147,483,648$ and $+2,147,483,648$.

You enforce referential integrity to protect against the accidental deletion of related records. A record in the primary table cannot be deleted if there is a matching record in the related table. Referential integrity will also disallow you from adding a record to the related table that does not have a matching record in the primary table. Furthermore, you cannot change the value of the primary key in the primary table if there is a matching record in the related table. All of this ensures that the relationships between records are valid and that the data in the related fields matches.

Figure 2-21 Defining the Employees/Position table relationship

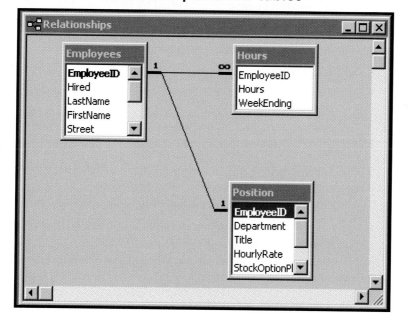

Access automatically creates the relationships based on the structure of the tables

Figure 2-22 Relationship between employees' hours and positions tables

Practice

Open the Relationships window in the Tuning Tracker database. Add the field lists for the Customers, Service Records, and Service History tables to the window. Create the one-to-one relationship between the CustomerID fields in the Customers and Service Records tables. Enforce referential integrity. Create the one-to-many relationship between the CustomerID field in the Customers and Service History tables. Enforce referential integrity. Close the window, saving the changes when prompted. Minimize the application window.

skill

Sorting and Finding Records

MOUS Skill

concept

Even though you enter records into a table in some kind of logical order, at some point you may need to work with your data in a different order. You can rearrange or sort the records in your tables according to any field you choose. You sort in either Ascending (A to Z, 1 to 10) or descending (Z to A, 10 to 1) order. You also can use the Find command to locate a specific data item within a table. For example you may want to find the record for a particular employee or a particular video.

do it!

Perform a sort on the Employees table in the Employees 2 database based on the Last Name field. Use the Find command to locate and edit a record.

1. Open the Employees table in the Employees 2 database in Datasheet View.

2. Either use the field selector to select the Last Name column or position the insertion point in any of the Last Name fields. Click the Sort Ascending button ⏷ on the Table Datasheet toolbar. The records are sorted by last name alphabetically from A to Z.

3. Click the Find button 🔍 on the Table Datasheet toolbar. The Find and Replace dialog box opens as shown in Figure 2-23. Access has automatically chosen to search within the selected field.

4. Type Van Pelt to replace the current selection in the Find What text box. Click Find Next .

5. The record containing the text Van Pelt is located and highlighted in the table. Click the Replace tab. Type Geddes, in the Replace with list box as shown in Figure 2-24. Click Replace to replace Van Pelt with the employee's new married name.

6. Van Pelt should be selected in the Find What list box. Type De. Click Find Next . A dialog box informs you that the search item was not found. Click OK . A whole field search will only locate an exact match with the Find What box.

7. Click the list arrow on the Match list box. Select Any Part of Field on the drop-down list. Click Find Next . Access selects the record for Adelman, which contains the De sequence in any part of the field. Continue clicking Find Next to view the other records that will be located with this search. Click OK to close the dialog box when the search is complete.

8. Click the list arrow on the Match list box. Select Start of Field on the drop down list. Press [Enter]. This time Access locates the record for DeBois. Press [Enter] again. There are no more records with the De sequence at the start of the field. Click OK and close the Find and Replace dialog box.

9. Close the Employees table. Click Yes to leave the table sorted alphabetically by last name.

more You can use wildcard characters as placeholders for other characters when you only know part of the value you want to find or you want to find values that begin with a certain letter or match a certain pattern. For example, you can enter st* to find start, still and stitch, or w?ll to find well, wall and will. Figure 2-25 explains the various wildcard symbols you can use to help you locate specific items of data. You can also check the Match Case check box to locate entries that match the uppercase and lowercase configuration of the text in the Find What list box.

Figure 2-23 Find tab in Find and Replace dialog box

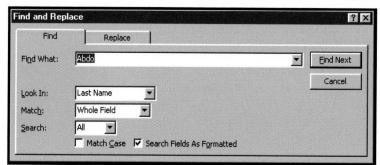

Figure 2-24 Replace tab in Find and Replace dialog box

Click to make search sensitive to uppercase and lowercase letters

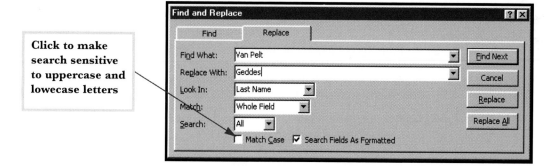

Figure 2-25 Wildcard characters used as search parameters

Wildcard	Used For	Example
*	Matching any number of characters; may be placed at the beginning, end, or in the middle of text	thr* finds throw, through, and thrush
?	Matching any single alphabetic character	t?n finds tan, ten, and tin, but not town
[ ]	Matching any single character within the brackets	t[ae]n finds tan and ten, but not tin
[!]	Matching any character not in the brackets	t[!ae]n finds tin and ton, but not tan or ten
[-]	Matching any one of a range of characters, specified in alphabetical order	ta[a-m] finds tab and tag, but not tan or tap
#	Matching any single numeric character	4#0 finds 410 and 420, but not 4110 or 415

Practice

Sort the Customers table in the Tuning Tracker database alphabetically by last name. Find the record for the person who lives on 38th St. Hint: You will have to select the appropriate field first and then use an Any Part of Field match. Save the change to the table design, close the table and minimize the application window.

skill

Filtering Records

concept

While sorting allows you to control the order in which records are displayed, filters control which records are displayed. Filtering temporarily narrows down the number of records according to criteria that you select. Records that do not meet your specifications are filtered out. A filter is a temporary subset of data that you can format and print. You can also save a filter as a permanent data subset by saving it as a query. A query is a subset of specific data that is extracted from a table or from another query.

do it!

Use Filter by Selection to isolate the records of employees who live in Elmsford. Filter by Form to create a data subset of all female employees who live in Irvington or Dobbs Ferry. Save this filter as a query.

1. Open the Employees table in the Employees 2 database. Click in any City field. Click ⤒ to sort the datasheet alphabetically by City.

2. To Filter by Selection you must locate an instance of the value you want the filtered records to contain. With the table sorted, you can easily locate and place the insertion point in one of the City fields containing the value Elmsford. Click in one of the City fields containing Elmsford.

3. Click the Filter by Selection button ⭟ on the Table Datasheet toolbar. Seven records are selected as shown in Figure 2-25. Filter by Selection is a quick and easy way to filter a datasheet based on the value in a single field.

4. Click the Remove Filter button ⭟ to display the full datasheet. ⬭ The Remove Filter button is really the same button as the Apply Filter button. The button is depressed and changes function when a filter is in effect.

5. Click the Filter by Form button ⬚ on the Table Datasheet toolbar. Click the list arrow in the City field. Select Irvington on the drop-down list.

6. Click in the Gender field. Click the list arrow and select F on the drop-down list. ⬭ This is an AND condition, Access will filter out all employees who live in Irvington and are female.

7. Click the Or tab in the bottom left hand corner of the Filter by Form window. Select F in the Gender field again.

8. Click in the City field. Click the list arrow and select Dobbs Ferry on the drop-down list.

9. Click the Apply Filter button ⬚ on the Filter/Sort toolbar. The four female employees from either Irvington or Dobbs Ferry are displayed as a data subset as shown in Figure 2-26.

10. Open the Records menu, point to Filter and click Advanced Filter/Sort on the Filter submenu. The details of the filter open in Design View as shown in Figure 2-27.

11. Click the Save as Query button ⬚ on the Filter/Sort toolbar. Type: Female, Irvington or Dobbs Ferry in the Query Name text box and click ⬚ OK ⬚.

12. Close the Design View window and the data subset. Click ⬚ No ⬚ when you are asked if you want to save the changes to the design of the table, so that you leave the datasheet sorted by Last Name rather than by City. Click Queries on the Objects bar to view the filter that you saved as a query in the queries list.

Figure 2-25 Filtering by Selection

		Employee ID	Hired	Last Name	First Name	Street	City	State	Zip	Gend
▶	+	41	8/1/1998	Castle	Frank	51 Stone Ave	Elmsford	NY	10523-	M
	+	31	)/27/1997	Young	Trent	77 Silver Rd	Elmsford	NY	10523-	M
	+	27	5/4/1996	Rush	Francis	2122 Lincoln Rd	Elmsford	NY	10523-	M
	+	23	7/2/1995	James	Arthur	89 Indian Bluff Blvd	Elmsford	NY	10523-	M
	+	19	4/19/1995	Rosafort	Lyle	1 Upland Ln	Elmsford	NY	10523-	M
	+	16	3/25/1994	Collins	Elmer	17 Cornell Ave	Elmsford	NY	10523-	M
	+	2	6/5/1993	Young	Tracy	665 Boylston St	Elmsford	NY	10523-	F

Record: ⏮ ◀   1   ▶ ⏭ ▶* of 7 (Filtered)

Figure 2-26 Filtering by Form

		Employee ID	Hired	Last Name	First Name	Street	City	State	Zip	Gender
▶	+	29	5/11/1996	Smith	Rhonda	11 Smith Ave	Dobbs Ferry	NY	10522-	F
	+	48	3/28/1999	Greco	Hannah	12 Woodland Ave.	Irvington	NY	10533-	F
	+	47	3/28/1999	McBride	Meghan	777 Pear Pl.	Irvington	NY	10533-	F
	+	24	)/21/1995	Harris	Stephanie	1431 Lakeview Cir.	Irvington	NY	10533-	F
✳		(AutoNumber)						NY		

Record: ⏮ ◀   1   ▶ ⏭ ▶* of 4 (Filtered)

Figure 2-27 Filter by Form in Design View

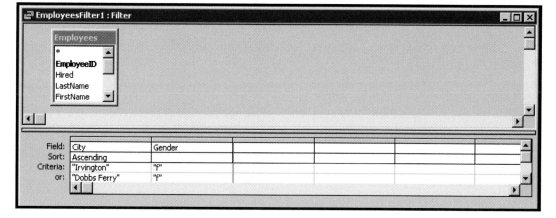

Field:	City	Gender			
Sort:	Ascending				
Criteria:	"Irvington"	"F"			
or:	"Dobbs Ferry"	"F"			

Practice

Open the Customers table in the Tuning Tracker database in Datasheet View. Sort the records in ascending order by zip code. Highlight an instance of the 10010 zip code and use Filter by Selection to display only the records of customers who live in that zip code. Remove the filter. Use Filter by Form to isolate the records of customers who live in 10010, Or 10011, Or 10012. Save the filter as a query named 10010, 10011, and 10012. Close the Design View window and the data subset. Do not save the changes to the table design. You want the records to remain sorted by last name not by zip code. Minimize the application window.

skill Using the Simple Query Wizard

 MOUS Skill

concept

A query is a formal way to sort and filter data. You can designate which fields you want and in what order you want them to appear. You can also specify separate filter criteria for each field and the order in which you want each field to be sorted. You can use queries to analyze your data. Queries are similar to filters in that they both create data subsets, but the important difference is that queries are saved as objects in the database. While a filter is a temporary view of the data, a query is a permanent data subset.

do it!

Create a query to answer the question: Which employees are on the company health plan?

1. With Queries selected on the Objects bar in the Employees 2 database, double-click Create query by using wizard in the Database window. The Simple Query Wizard opens.

2. With Table: Employees selected in the Table/Queries list box, click EmployeeID, if necessary, in the Available Fields scrolling list box. Click ⟩ to add the field to the Selected Fields box.

3. Select Last Name in the Available Fields scrolling list box. Click ⟩ to add it to the Selected Fields box. Follow the same procedure to add the First Name field.

4. Click the list arrow on the Table/Queries list box. Select Table: Position on the drop-down list. Add the Department, Title, and Health Plan fields to the Selected Fields box. The dialog box should look like Figure 2-28. Click Next > .

5. Leave the Detail (shows every field for every record) option button selected and click Next > .

6. A suggested query title is selected for modification. Type: Health Plan Query. Click Finish .

7. The query is created and opened in Datasheet View. Click 📝 ▾ on the Query Datasheet toolbar to switch to Query Design View.

8. The top half of the Query design grid displays the field lists for the tables from which you have selected fields and the relationship between the tables. The bottom half displays each field you have selected for the query and which table it is in, and provides cells in which you can choose the sort order, choose to display or hide the field in the query, and set criteria for which records to extract.

(continued on AC 2.26)

Figure 2-28 Selecting Fields for the Query in the Simple Query Wizard dialog

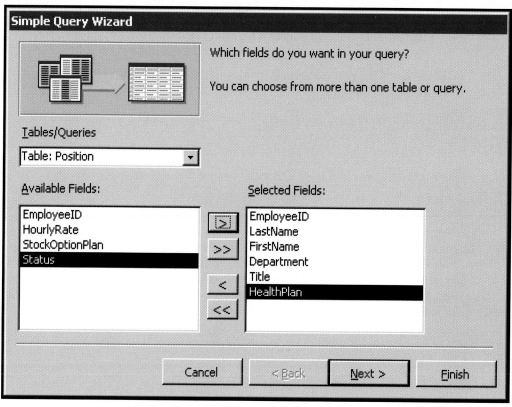

skill Using the Simple Query Wizard (cont'd)

do it!

9. Click in the Sort cell for the Last Name field. Click the list arrow and select Ascending. Click in the Sort cell for the First Name cell. Click the list arrow and select Ascending. This is the secondary sort field for the datasheet. In cases where two employees have the same last name, the records will be sorted alphabetically based on the first name.

10. Click in the Criteria cell for the Health Plan field. Type: Yes. The Query design grid is shown in Figure 2-29.

11. Click the Run button  on the Query Design toolbar. The records for all employees on the company health plan are displayed in alphabetical order (see Figure 2-30). Notice that Collins, Elmer is listed before Collins, John.

12. Save the changes to the design of the query and close the datasheet.

more

The Simple Query Wizard creates a simple Select query. Select queries retrieve and display records in Datasheet View. Select queries are the most common type of query, but you will learn in later lessons how to create several kinds of action queries. Action queries create new tables or modify data in existing tables. There are four types of Action queries: Make-table, Append, Delete and Update. Append queries add new records to tables and Delete queries delete records from tables that correspond to the rows of the query result set. Update queries change the values of existing fields in a table corresponding to rows of the query result set. For example, you can raise the salaries for people in a certain job category by 3%. You will also learn how to create a Parameter query, which is a flexible query that is used over and over again with simple changes made to its criteria each time it is run. Each time you run a parameter query, Access displays a dialog box that prompts you for the new criterion.

Figure 2-29 Sorting and Adding Criteria to the filter

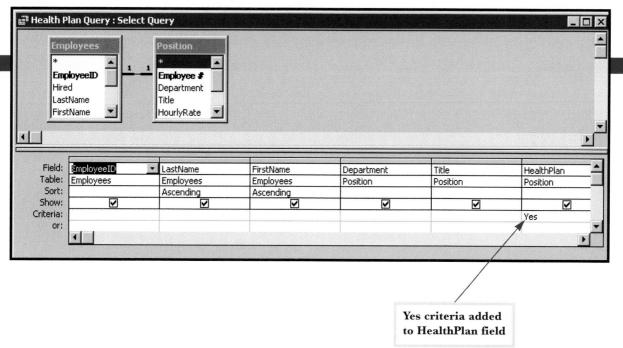

Yes criteria added
to HealthPlan field

Figure 2-30 Employees on health plan listed alphabetically

Employee ID	Last Name	First Name	Department	Title	Health Plan
14	Abdo	Muhammad	Purchasing	Purchaser	☑
38	Adelman	Jody	Purchasing	Secretary	☑
35	Alvarez	Alex	Operations	Data Entry Clerk	☑
39	Borda	Ella	Sales	Account Manager	☑
1	Busing	Klaus	Operations	Supervisor	☑
49	Caruso	Maria	Sales	Secretary	☑
41	Castle	Frank	Purchasing	Purchaser	☑
9	Chandler	Kevin	Operations	File Clerk	☑
26	Chung	Jill	Warehouse	Inventory Control	☑
16	Collins	Elmer	Shipping & Receiving	Security	☑
33	Collins	John	Warehouse	Shipping Manager	☑
45	DeBois	Kirby	Sales	Account Manager	☑
50	Geddes	Laura	Shipping & Receiving	Shipping Manager	☑

Record: 1 of 43

Practice

In the Tuning Tracker database, create a query to answer the question: How many customers have not had their pianos tuned in 2 years? Use the Simple Query Wizard to add the Customer ID, Last Name, and Last Tuned fields to the query. Open the query in Design View. In the Criteria cell for the Last Tuned field, enter the expression that will isolate the correct records. For example, if today's date is 9/30/01, enter < 9/30/99. Run the query, save it as 2 Years, and close the datasheet. Minimize the application window.

skill
Creating a Calculated Field in a Query

concept

A calculated field uses data in one or more fields to create a new field. Arithmetic operators and functions can be used to perform calculations on data already included in your database. When you create a new field based on existing database fields, always use a query rather than defining a new field in a table in Design View. This will ensure that the new field updates as data is added and changed in the related tables.

do it!

Create a query to answer the question: What is the gross pay each week for every employee?

1. With Queries selected on the Objects bar in the Employees 2 Database window, double-click Create query by using wizard.

2. Create a query using the Employee ID, Last Name and First Name fields from the Employees table, the Hours and Week Ending fields from the Hours table, and the Hourly Rate field from the Position table.

3. You want the query to show every field from every record. Name the query Gross Weekly Pay and open it in Design View.

4. The thin gray box at the top of each column in the bottom half of the design grid is the column selector. Hover the mouse pointer over one of the column selectors until it becomes a small black arrow. Click to select the column. Click anywhere else in the Design grid to cancel the selection.

5. Hover the mouse pointer over the gridline on the right side of the first empty column. (This will be the seventh field in the datasheet.) When the pointer becomes a horizontal resizing pointer, drag to the right to increase the width of the column and create a clear space to complete the following steps (see Figure 2-31).

6. Click in the Field cell for the column you just widened. Type: Gross Weekly Pay:. This will be the column heading for the calculated field.

7. In the same cell, continue typing CCur([Hours]*[HourlyRate]). This will multiply the Hours worked each week by the employee's hourly pay. ◖◗ Make sure to include the colon following the field name, and not to use a space in the Hourly Rate field name.

   ◖◗ The function CCur converts a numeric value to a Currency data type.

8. In the Show cells for the Hours and Hourly Rate fields, click the check boxes to clear the selection. This will hide the two fields in Datasheet View. Check your design grid with Figure 2-32.

9. Click the Run button 🖽 on the Query Design toolbar to run the query. The query with the gross weekly pay calculation opens as shown in Figure 2-32.

10. Close the datasheet, saving the changes to the design when prompted. Complete the Practice session and exit Access.

more

The * operator is used for multiplication. You use the +, –, /, and ^ operators to perform addition, subtraction, division, and exponentiation. Fields which are having calculations performed on them must be enclosed in brackets. The parentheses must surround the calculation so that the function CCur is performed on the result. The colon must be included after the field name to indicate that an expression will follow. If you do not type a field name Access will enter the default Expr1 as the calculated field name.

You can drag a selected column in the Query design grid to change the order for the fields in the query. To delete a field, select it and either press the [Delete] key or click the Delete command on the Edit menu. When you remove a field from the design grid you are only removing it from the query stipulations, the field and the data it contains are secure in the under-lying table.

Figure 2-31 Creating a Calculated Field

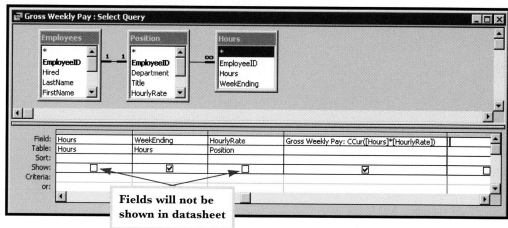

Figure 2-32 Gross Weekly Pay Query

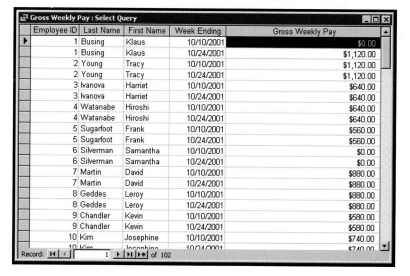

Practice

In the Tuning Tracker database, create a query to answer the question: How old are our customer's pianos. Use the Simple Query Wizard to collect the Customer ID, Piano Make, Piano Model and Year fields from the Service Records table. Save the query as Customer's Piano Age and open it in Design View. Create a calculated field named Piano Age using the expression, "Current Year"-[Year]. For example if the year is 2002, enter the expression "2002" - [Year]. Run the query. The piano with an unknown age will return an error message. Save the change to the query design and close the application window.

shortcuts

Function	Button/Mouse	Menu	Keyboard
Create a new database		Click File, then click New	[Ctrl]+[N]
Set primary key		In Table Design View, click Edit, then click Primary Key	[Alt]+[E], [K]
Open the Show Table dialog box	On the Relationships toolbar	With the Relationships window open, click Relationships, then click Show Table	[Alt]+[R], [T]
Sort records in ascending order		Click Records, point to Sort, then click Sort Ascending	[Alt]+[R], [S], [A]
Find an item of data		Click Edit, then click Find	[Ctrl]+[F]
Filter By Selection		Click Records, point to Filter, then click Filter by Selection	[Alt]+[R], [F], [S]
Apply Filter/Remove Filter		Click Records, then click Apply Filter/Sort or Remove Filter/Sort	[Alt]+[R], [Y] or [Alt]+[R], [R]
Filter By Form		Click Records, point to Filter, then click Filter by Form	[Alt]+[R], [F], [F]
Save As Query		In the Filter By Form window, click File, then click Save As Query	[Alt]+[F], [A]
Run a query		In Query Design View, click Query, then click Run	[Alt]+[Q], [R]

A. Identify Key Features

Name the items indicated by callouts in Figure 2-33.

Figure 2-33 Employees table in Datasheet View

1.
2.
3.
4.
5.
6.
7.

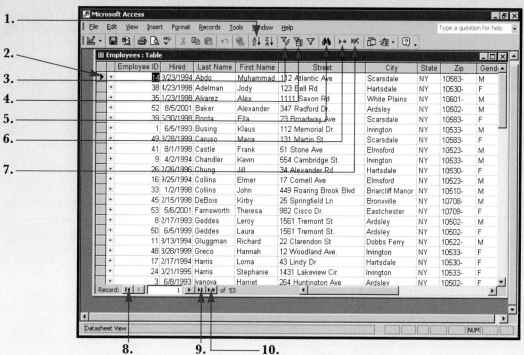

8.
9.
10.

B. Select the Best Answer

11. This is a custom window that contains command buttons for opening the objects in the database that a user is most likely to need.

12. You set this property to choose the format for a Yes/No field

13. You set this property to automatically enter the value the user is most likely to enter in a field

14. This property controls the text that displays in the Field selector in Datasheet View

15. This is a character string that determines how data will be entered and displayed in a field and how it will be stored in the database

16. This is a short expression that will test the reasonableness of an entry

17. This is used to ensure that the relationships between records are valid and that the data in the related fields matches

18. You can use this as a placeholder for other characters when you only know part of the value you want to find in a datasheet

19. This is a temporary subset of data that you can format and print

20. This is a permanent data subset that is saved as an object in the database

a. Input mask

b. Default Value

c. Validation rule

d. Query

e. Switchboard

f. Wildcard character

g. Filter

h. Caption

i. Display Control

j. Referential Integrity

quiz (continued)

C. Complete the Statement

21. This symbol in the Format property for a Text field instructs the program to capitalize the entries in the field

   a. <

   b. +

   c. >

   d. ~

22. These temporarily narrow down the number of records that are displayed according to criteria that you select.

   a. Sorts

   b. Queries

   c. Properties

   d. Filters

23. These allow you to control the order in which records are displayed.

   a. Sorts

   b. Queries

   c. Properties

   d. Filters

24. These are used to answer questions about the data in a database and are saved as objects in the database.

   a. Sorts

   b. Queries

   c. Properties

   d. Filters

25. For programming purposes, you should enter the field names:

   a. With quotation marks surrounding them

   b. Without spaces or with underscores between words

   c. With all capital letters

   d. With slash marks to indicate literal characters

26. The field descriptions will display:

   a. In the error message when a validation rule has been broken

   b. In a ScreenTip when you hover the mouse pointer over the Field selector

   c. In the Status bar in Datasheet View when the field is selected

   d. Only in the Description cell in the Design View grid

27. The field you will use to link the records in the primary table to records in other tables is called:

   a. A principal join

   b. A composite key

   c. An AutoNumber field

   d. A primary key

28. You set the Field Size property for a Number field to:

   a. Change the number of characters allowed in the field

   b. Raise or lower the amount of storage space the field will require in the memory of the computer

   c. Format the field as a General number, or as a Fixed decimal, Percent or Currency value

   d. Designate the number of decimal places you want in the field

29. When you create a calculated field based on existing database fields you should do all of the following except always:

   a. Use brackets around the field names

   b. Use a query rather than defining a new field in a table in Design View

   c. Create the expression in the Display Control property in Table design view.

   d. Include a colon after the name for the calculated field, before you enter the expression

interactivity

Build Your Skills

1. Create a new database and use the Table Wizard to construct the first table

   a. Start Access and click Blank Database on the task pane. Name the new database Address Book.mdb.

   b. Use the Table Wizard to create the Addresses table in the Personal category. Use the AddressID, LastName, FirstName, SpouseName, Address, City, StateOrProvince and PostalCode fields. Use the Rename Field button to rename the StateOrProvince field, State, and the PostalCode field ZipCode.

   c. Let Access set the AddressID field as the primary key for you and open the table in Design View.

2. Modify the field properties for the new table.

   a. Decrease the field sizes for the Last Name and First Name fields to 25 each. Decrease the size of the Address field to 50. Decrease the ZipCode field to 10 characters.

   b. Make the State field 2 characters long and format it in uppercase letters. Enter your state as the default value for the field. Enter a description for the field.

   c. Enter Zip Code as the Caption property for the ZipCode field.

3. Create an input mask and add a data validation rule.

   a. Use the Input Mask Wizard to create a mask for the Zip Code field. Store the data with the symbols in the mask.

   b. Add a Text field for Gender. Set the field size to 1. Format the field as a capital letter.

   c. Set the data validation rule so that the field will only accept m or f.

   d. Enter validation text to display in the error dialog box.

   e. Save the changes and test the rule.

   f. Enter data for 5 people you know in the table and close the datasheet.

4. Create tables in Design View.

   a. Create a new table in Design View named Communication in the Address Book database. Create a Number field for the AddressID. Leave it in the default Long Integer format.

   b. Create a Text field for EMailAddress. Create a Text field for PhoneNumber and apply an input mask. Decrease the field size for the Phone Number field to 15. When you save the table do NOT set a primary key. You may enter several e-mail addresses or phone numbers for each Address ID. This will be the many side of the relationship.

   c. Enter the data for the 5 people you have in the Addresses table with the matching Address ID. Make sure you enter two e-mail addresses and/or two phone numbers for at least some of the entries. Close the datasheet.

   d. Create another new table named Contact Details. Create a Number primary key field for the AddressID field. Create a field called Relationship. Use the Lookup Wizard to create a value list with the choices: Acquaintance, Business Contact, Friend, and Relative. Decrease the field size to accommodate the longest entry in the list. Save the changes.

interactivity (continued)

Build Your Skills (continued)

e. Create a Yes/No field named VisitScheduled. Enter the Caption properties for each field as necessary. Add a Date/Time field named Birthday. Apply the Long Date format. Save the changes.

f. Create a field called TimesCalledperMonth. Create a value list with the choices: 1–3, 4–6, 7–9. Decrease the field size appropriately and save the changes. Switch to Datasheet View, increase the column widths and save the changes. Enter data in the table and close the datasheet.

g. Establish the One-to-Many relationship between the AddressID fields in the Addresses and Communications tables and the One-to-One relationship between the Contact Details and Addresses tables. Enforce referential integrity and save the changes.

5. Create queries.

a. Use the Simple Query Wizard to create a permanent data subset to answer the question: Which of my contacts are friends? Include the Last Name, First Name, and Relationship fields. Name the query Friends and open it in Design View.

b. In the Criteria cell for the Relationship field type: friend. Press [Enter], run the query, and save the changes. Close the Address Book database.

6. Open the Home Video Collection database. Use the Simple Query Wizard to create a query to answer the question: Which of my videos are rated PG-13? Use the Title, Genre and Rating fields, name it PG-13, and open it in Design View. Type: PG-13, in the Criteria cell for the Rating field. Press [Enter], run the query, and save the changes. Close the database.

7. Open the Recipes database. Use the Simple Query Wizard to answer the question: Which of my recipes can be created in half an hour or less? Use the Recipe Name, Which Meal? and Time to Prepare fields. Name the query Quick Recipes and open it in Design View. Type: <31 in the Criteria cell for the Time to Prepare field. Press [Enter], run the query, and save the changes. Fill in the Which Meal fields as necessary. Open the Recipes table to see that these fields have been entered in the underlying table. Close the database.

Problem Solving Exercises

1. Build the Magazine Preferences database that you outlined on paper for Lesson 1. Begin a Blank database and name it Magazine Preferences. Construct the three tables you planned in Design View. Assign appropriate data types and field sizes. Make sure not to duplicate any fields. Follow database programming principles when you name the fields and enter Caption properties as necessary. Use the most efficient Byte field size for the Age and Number of Magazines Read Regularly fields. Make sure you use the Auto Number and Number data type in the Long Integer size for the fields you will use to establish relationships. Set the primary keys. The table containing the Hobbies field will not have a primary key. It will be on the many side of the relationship. You will be able to enter several hobbies for each survey respondent.

2. Format the Gender field so that it appears as 1 uppercase letter. Create an input mask for the Social Security field. Create a data validation rule and validation text for the Gender field. Save and name each table. Switch to Datasheet View for each table and enter the data you have compiled. Adjust the column widths as necessary. Apply formatting to the datasheet for the primary table.

interactivity (continued)

Problem Solving Exercises (continued)

3. Establish the table relationships. You should have one one-to-one relationship and one one-to-many relationship. Enforce referential integrity. Sort the records in the primary table in descending order by age. Filter by Selection to display a subset of only the female survey respondents. Filter by Form to display a subset of records for survey respondents who are Female AND 22 OR Female AND 23 OR Female AND 24.

4. Create queries using the Simple Query wizard to answer the questions: How many survey respondents are between the ages of 18 and 34 (>18 And <34), between the ages of 35 and 49 (>35 And <49), between the ages of 50 and 64 (>50 And <64), and over 65 (>65). Include the ID #, Occupation, # of Magazines Read Regularly, Age, and Gender fields in each query and then set the appropriate criteria in the Age field. If these age groups are not represented in your data you can use other criteria for example under 17 (<17), 18 to 25 (>18 And <25) or 26 to 34 (>26 And <34) etc. Save each query with the age group name.

three

3

Creating Forms

- ⚡ **Creating an AutoForm**

- ⚡ **Creating a Form with the Form Wizard**

- ⚡ **Modifying a Form**

- ⚡ **Setting Tab Order**

- ⚡ **Adding a Field to a Form**

- ⚡ **Using the Expression Builder**

- ⚡ **Using Property Sheets**

- ⚡ **Entering Records Using a Form**

As you have seen, tables serve as the backbone of a database, and you can enter your data directly into them. However, after you have tested your database design by adding sample data to your tables, you will want to build forms to simplify data entry. Forms will serve as the user interface for your database. Although you can use Datasheet View in either a table or a query to access, edit and add data, a form will provide a more user friendly environment. Forms are constructed from any number of objects called controls or control objects. You use text box controls for entering and editing data. Label controls are used to identify the text boxes and other control objects, and toggle button, option button, or checkbox controls are used for Yes/No fields.

Using a form you can enter data into several tables at once. More importantly, you can choose a format that displays only one record at a time to simplify data entry and reduce errors. There are three ways to create a form. The easiest way to create a form is with an AutoForm Wizard. If you simply want a form that displays all of the records from a single table or query, you can let Access create a standardized form for you. AutoForm is the least flexible but quickest way to create a form.

The Form Wizard enables you to create a form by following a series of dialog boxes and choosing which fields to include. The Form Wizard offers less control than creating a form on your own, but it is much faster. One advantage to using the Form Wizard is that you can choose fields from more than one table creating a form that will enable users to enter data into several tables simultaneously. Finally, you can create a form in Form Design View. You will have more control over where to put each field and how to format the fields, but it is the most complicated method. In the Form Design window you add the dynamic controls that you will use to enter and edit data and the static controls that will hold the identifying labels and titles.

There are three types of form controls. Bound controls are fields containing data from a table or query. There must be a bound control for each field you want to be able to enter data into. Labels and titles are unbound controls. Unbound controls are the identifiers that tell the user what data to enter where. Calculated controls display values created from expressions. You can use calculated controls to include totals, subtotals, averages, percentages, or date calculations. If you use a value in the expression that is stored in one of the other data fields, the calculated control will be bound to that field. Otherwise it will be an unbound control. In other words, the term bound indicates a link to a field in a table.

Lesson Goal:

Create an AutoForm. Create a form with the Form Wizard. Modify and format form controls. Create a calculated control and add records using a form.

Access 2002

skill

Creating an AutoForm MOUS Skill

concept

To create a simple form that only includes the fields from a single table or query you can use an AutoForm Wizard. AutoForm Columnar is the most popular format because it creates a form that aligns the fields in columns with each record displayed individually. This is the advantage of creating a columnar form. You can use the navigation buttons at the bottom of the form to scroll through the data, one record per screen, to locate, view, and edit records individually.

do it!

Create an AutoForm to enter data into the Employees table.

1. Start Access and open the Employees 2 database. Click Forms on the Objects bar to display the options for creating a form in the objects list.

2. Click ⊞ New on the Database Window toolbar. The New Form dialog box opens.

3. Click AutoForm: Columnar. Click the list arrow on the box with the instructions: Choose the table or query where the object's data comes from, as shown in Figure 3-1.

4. Click Employees on the drop-down list to select this table as the record source for the form. The record source is the table or query where you are getting the data for the form. Click OK.

5. A standard columnar form is created with all of the fields from the Employees table, as shown in Figure 3-2. The fields are created in the same order as in the datasheet.

6. Use the navigation buttons at the bottom of the form to view the records in the form. Close the form without saving it. ◆ All Form Wizards "remember" the previous styles you have applied. The last autoformat that was used to create a form will be used by the AutoForm Wizard.

more

You can choose from three basic AutoForm formats: columnar, tabular, or datasheet. In a tabular form, the fields in each record appear on one line with the labels displayed once, at the top of the form, as shown in Figure 3-3. In a datasheet form, the fields in each record appear in row and column format with one record in each row and one field in each column. The field names appear at the top of the column, just like in a table. Pivot table forms are used to create forms from Excel pivot tables.

You can also create a columnar AutoForm based on the record source that is selected in the Database window. For example, with Queries selected on the Objects bar, you can select the Health Plan query in the Database window. Then you can open the Insert menu and select the AutoForm command to automatically create a form that includes all of the fields in the query. You can also click the list arrow on the New Object button on the Database toolbar and select the AutoForm command. The New Object button displays the last object you created. For example, if the last object you created was an AutoForm, the New Object: AutoForm button ▣ displays.

Figure 3-1 Creating an AutoForm

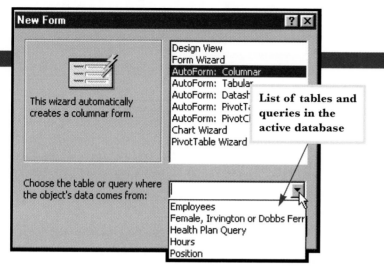

Figure 3-2 A Columnar AutoForm

Figure 3-3 A Tabular AutoForm

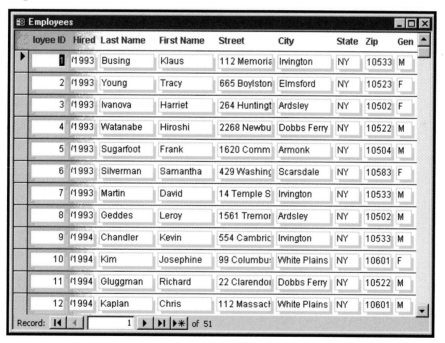

Practice

Open a second Access application window. Open the Tuning Tracker 2 database in your Access Student Files folder. The phone numbers have been entered in the Customers table and the Service History table has been completed. Create a columnar AutoForm for entering records into the Customers table. Save it as Customers AutoForm and minimize the application window.

skill

Creating a Form with the Form Wizard

concept

As you have seen, your options are limited when you create an AutoForm. If you want to change the layout, choose a background template, or choose fields from several different tables, you should use the Form Wizard to create your form. The Form Wizard provides a compromise between the ease of the AutoForm and the total control of designing a form in Design View. You can use the Form Wizard to quickly create a form and then modify its properties in the Design View window.

do it!

Create a form to enter the data into the Employees and Positions tables.

1. In the Employees 2 database window, click Forms on the Objects bar. Double-click Create form by using wizard in the database window. The first Form Wizard dialog box opens.

2. Table: Employees should be selected from the Tables/Queries list box. If it is not, click the list arrow and select it from the drop-down list.

3. Click the Select All Fields button `>>` to move all the Available Fields to the Selected Fields box.

4. Click the list arrow on the Tables/Queries list box. Select Table: Position from the drop-down list. Click `>>`.

5. Select the Position.EmployeeID field in the Selected Fields box. Click the Remove Field button `<`. The EmployeeID field has already been added to the form from the Employees table. The Selected Fields box is shown in Figure 3-4. Click `Next >`.

6. Leave the Columnar option button selected, and click `Next >`.

7. Click Blends to choose it as the style for your report. Click `Next >`.

8. Type: Employees/Position as the title for the form. Leave the Open the form to view or enter information option button selected and click `Finish`.

9. The Form is created and saved and opens in Form View as shown in Figure 3-5. Notice that the Yes/No fields from the tables are check box controls on the form and the drop-down value list you created with the Lookup Wizard is a combo box control. The rest of the form controls are either text boxes or labels.

more

The main advantage to using the Form Wizard is that you can choose fields from several tables. You can choose the fields you want to include from as many different tables or queries as you want. When choosing fields from several different record sources, be sure not to duplicate the shared fields. Generally you will include all of the fields from several tables so that the form can be used to easily enter data into more than one table at the same time.

Figure 3-4 Choosing the fields for the form

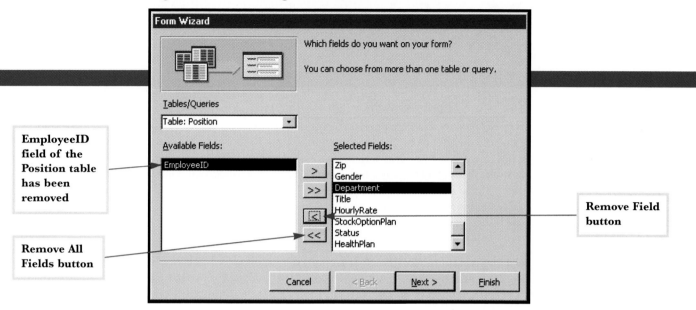

EmployeeID
field of the
Position table
has been
removed

Remove All
Fields button

Remove Field
button

Figure 3-5 Employees/Position form

Modified form
opened in Form View

Practice

In the Tuning Tracker 2 database, use the Form Wizard to create a form for entering records into the Customers and Service Records tables. Make sure you remove the duplicate CustomerID field from the Selected Fields box. Use a columnar layout and the SandStone style. Name it Customers/Service Records. Close the form and minimize the application window.

skill

Modifying a Form

concept

Even if you choose to create your forms using a Wizard, you can make changes in Design View to manually tweak your forms into exactly the format you need. You can make the form easier to work with by rearranging the layout and resizing the fields. You can also apply borders and shading, change the text color or text style for certain controls, and apply other formatting changes to make your forms visually appealing.

do it!

Modify the control properties for the Employees/Position form.

1. Open the Employees/Position form in the Employees 2 database in Design View. Since you will not be adding any new controls yet, you can close the Toolbox either by clicking its close button or by clicking the Toolbox button ⚒ on the Form Design toolbar to toggle it off.

2. Drag the lower-right corner of the Form window downward and to the right to reveal the entire form. Release the mouse button when you can see the Form Footer. ◖◗ There are two components to every field, the text box control and the corresponding static, unbound label control.

3. Click the EmployeeID text box as shown in Figure 3-6. Sizing handles surround the selected object. Hover the mouse pointer over the border of the bound text box control; it becomes an open hand. You can use this pointer to move both the bound text box control and its corresponding unbound label control together as a unit.

4. Hover the mouse pointer over the black box in the upper-left corner of the text box control. This is called the move handle. As you can see, the move handles are larger than the sizing handles. The pointer becomes a hand with an extended finger. You can use this pointer to move an individual control.

5. Hover the mouse pointer over the midpoint sizing handle on the right end of the EmployeesID text box. When the pointer becomes a horizontal resizing arrow, drag to the left to the 1¾ inch mark on the horizontal ruler to decrease the size of the text box.

6. Click the HourlyRate text box to select it. Press [Shift] on the keyboard and click the Status combo box. Drag the midpoint resizing handle on the right end of either control to the 4¾ inch mark on the horizontal ruler to decrease the size of both controls at the same time. ◖◗ The Object list box, at the left end of the Formatting (Form/Report) toolbar, lists every control on the form. You can also click the name of an object on the drop-down list to select the corresponding control on the form.

7. Click 🖻 to switch to Form View and make sure the control are sized correctly. Make sure the longest entry in the combo box will be visible in Form View. Then click 📐 to switch back to Design View.

8. Drag the midpint sizing handle on the right end of the Department text box to the 5¼ inch mark on the horizontal ruler. Drag the right midpoint sizing handle on the Title text box to the 5⅛ mark. Drag the right midpoint sizing handle on the Last Name and First Name text boxes to the 2¼ mark. Make sure that the longest entry fits in the text boxes in Form View.

9. Select and move the Gender field (both the text box and its label) so that it is positioned underneath the Health Plan field as shown in Figure 3-7.

(continued on AC 3.8)

Figure 3-6 Form Design View window

Move handle

Sizing handles

EmployeeID
text box control

Label controls
(unbound)

Text box controls
(bound)

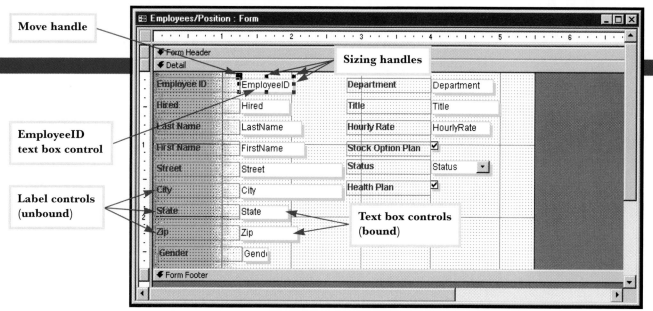

Figure 3-7 Moving the Gender field

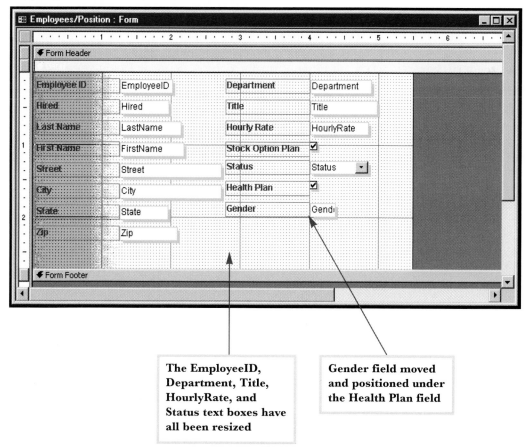

The EmployeeID,
Department, Title,
HourlyRate, and
Status text boxes have
all been resized

Gender field moved
and positioned under
the Health Plan field

skill

Modifying a Form (cont'd)

do it!

10. Select the EmployeeID text box. Press [Shift] and click each text box control on the form. Click the list arrow on the Line/Border Width button ⬚▾ on the Form Design toolbar. Change the border width for the controls to 2 as shown in Figure 3-8.

11. With all of the controls still selected, click the list arrow on the Font/Fore Color button 🅰▾. Change the font color for the controls to dark blue (the sixth square in the first row on the color palette).

12. Click a blank area of the form to cancel of the selection of the controls. Select the Hired text box. Click the list arrow on the Font list box and change the font to Courier. Click the list arrow on the Fill/Back Color button 🎨▾. Change the background color for the control to the lightest yellow.

13. Now change the back color for the control to Transparent. Switch to Form View. The background looks white. Select the Hired field. The background changes to the light yellow color when the field is selected as shown in Figure 3-9.

14. Save the changes to the design of the form and close the form.

more

The Bold, Italic, and Underline buttons modify the style of the selected text. The three alignment buttons, Align Left, Center, and Align Right, control the placement of text within a text box or label control. The last button on the Formatting toolbar is the Special Effects buttons, which controls the appearance of the outlines of a label or text box. You can choose a Raised, Sunken, Chiseled, Shadowed, or Etched effect. The Blends style uses a shadowed border effect.

Don't worry too much about resizing and moving your controls so that they are perfectly aligned. It is a very precise procedure, which requires excellent mouse skills. You will become better at it with practice. Just make sure that you understand which are the sizing-handles and which are the move-handles and that the open hand mouse pointer moves the text box and label control as a unit, while the extended finger mouse pointer moves the controls separately.

Figure 3-8 Changing the Border Style for selected controls

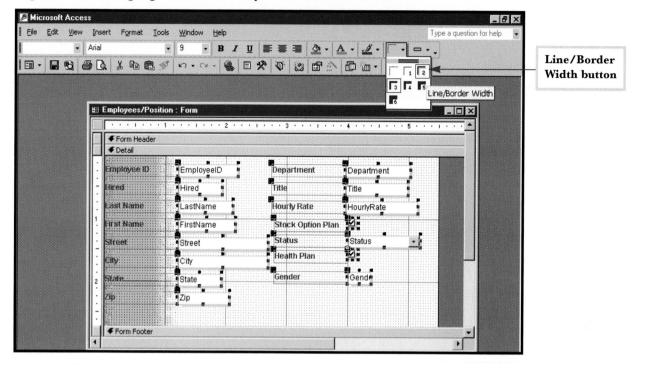

Line/Border Width button

Figure 3-9 Changing the Background color for a control when it is selected

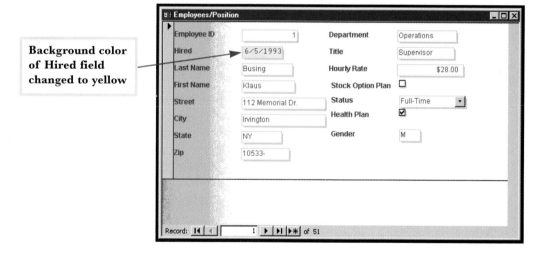

Background color of Hired field changed to yellow

Practice

Open the Customers/Service Records form in the Tuning Tracker 2 database in Design View. Decrease the sizes of the text boxes, making sure that the longest entry fits in Form View. Decrease the size of the Piano Make and Piano Model label controls. Move the Year, Use, and Last Tuned fields downward. Move the Piano Make and Piano Model fields into the space you create so that the fields from the Service Records table are the second column in the form. Use the appropriate pointers to align the labels and text boxes. Select all of the text box controls in the Customers/Service Records form. Apply a 2 pt border with a Shadowed special effect. Change the font in the Piano Make text box to Bookman Old Style and apply a bold font style. Move the Last Tuned field so that it is directly below the Piano Model field. Save the changes and minimize the window.

skill   Setting Tab Order

concept

Tab order refers to the sequence in which controls receive the focus when a user is pressing the Tab key to move through a form. When you first create a columnar form, the Tab order runs from top to bottom according to the order in which the fields were added to the form. When you move and rearrange fields, the Tab order does not automatically change. You can adjust the Tab order for your form so that users will be able to quickly and accurately enter data in a logical order.

do it!

Change the tab order for the Employees/Position form so that the moved Gender field will be last in the tab order. Set the Tab stop property for the State field.

1. Open the Employees/Position form in the Employees 2 database in Form View. Press the [Tab] key to tab through the controls on the form. You can see that the Gender field is not in the correct order.

2. Switch to Form Design View. Open the View menu and click the Tab Order command to open the Tab Order dialog box as shown in Figure 3-10.

3. Click the Gender row selector button as shown in Figure 3-10. Drag the Gender field to the bottom of the fields in the Custom Order scrolling list box. The Tab order is now set to move the focus down the first column of fields and then down the second column. You can click the Auto Order button to instruct Access to automatically set the tab order. The focus will start in the upper-left corner of the form and move across the first line. Then it will move down and proceed from left to right again.

4. Click [OK] to close the Tab Order dialog box.

5. Since NY has been entered as the default value for the State text box and very few employees live out of state, data entry personnel will rarely need to stop at this control. To increase data entry efficiency, you can set the Tab Stop property for the control to No so that the focus will skip the State text box. Click the State text box to select it.

6. Click the Properties button [icon] on the Form Design toolbar. A window with Text Box: State in the Title bar opens. This is the property sheet for the State text box.

7. Click the Other tab. You can now easily locate the Tab Stop property. Click in the Tab Stop property settings box. Click the list arrow and select No on the drop-down list as shown in Figure 3-11. Controls whose Tab Order property has been set to No can still be selected and edited in the form; they will simply never receive the focus as the user tabs through the form.

8. Click the Close button [X] to close the property sheet. Save the changes to the form design.

9. Switch to Form View and press [Tab] to tab through the form controls. The Gender field is now last in the tab order and the State field is skipped. Close the form. The Enter and arrow keys also respond to the new tab order. The focus will correctly shift to the controls you have specified when the user presses these keys to move through the fields in the form.

more

Remember that moving and rearranging the order of fields in a form will not automatically change the tab order. Tab order will have to be adjusted to reflect the new form structure. You can also change the tab order to suit your particular needs. For example, if you find that one field requires more editing than the others, you might want to put it first on the tab order without changing its location on the form. Or if a large number of the records you enter skip several fields, you might want to put those fields last in the tab order instead of changing their Tab Stop properties to No so that they can still be easily skipped.

Figure 3-10 Tab Order dialog box

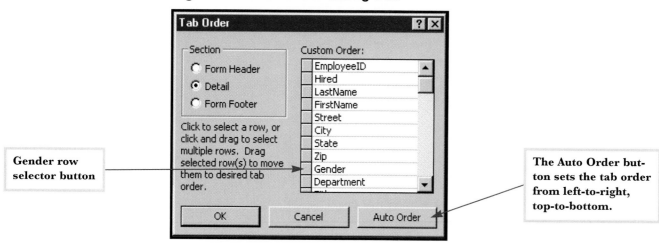

Gender row selector button

The Auto Order button sets the tab order from left-to-right, top-to-bottom.

Figure 3-11 Setting the Tab Stop property

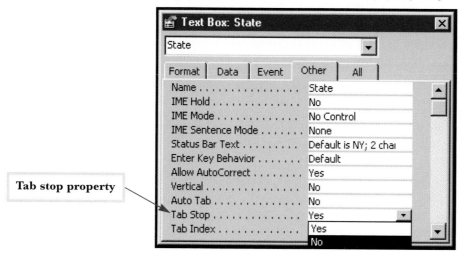

Tab stop property

Practice

Open the Customers/Service Records form in the Tuning Tracker 2 database in Design View. Open the Tab Order dialog box and move the Last Tuned field so that it is after the Piano Model field in the tab order to conform to its new position on the form. Save the change and test the tab order in Form View. Close the form and minimize the application window.

skill　Adding a Field to a Form

concept

You can use the Toolbox to add a field to your form that is not in the original record source/s. This type of text box is called an unbound control because it is not linked or bound to a field in a table or query. All of the text boxes in the form so far are bound controls. Each field in the form is linked to a field in the Employees or Position table. Unbound text boxes can be used to supply values to other fields or to display the results of calculations.

do it!

Use the Toolbox to add an unbound text box to the form.

1. Open the Employee/Position form in the Employees 2 database in Design View. Click the Toolbox button ⚒ on the Form Design toolbar.

2. Select the Last Name text box. Press [Shift] and select the First Name, Street, City, State and Zip text boxes. Move the selected block of controls down on the form to make room for a new text box.

3. Click the Text Box button 🔲 on the Toolbox. Move the mouse pointer over the form. The pointer becomes the symbol for the Text Box button combined with a crosshair. The center of the crosshair will define the position of the upper-left corner of the text box.

4. Click once directly below and aligned with the Hired text box to insert a text box with the word Unbound and a label that says Text: 30 as shown in Figure 3-12. ◖▬▬ The label caption (Text: 30) will vary depending on how many controls are on the form. This is the thirtieth control added to the Employees/Position form.

5. Drag one of the midpoint sizing-handles on the top or bottom of the text box to increase the width to match the Hired text box. Decrease the length to match the Hired text box.

6. With the two controls, the text box and its corresponding label, still selected, move the mouse pointer over the move handle in the upper left-hand corner of the label. When the mouse pointer becomes a hand with a pointing finger, drag to move the label into position below the Hired label.

7. Click the Text: 30 label to select it, and use the sizing handles to adjust the width to match the Hired label. Double-click the label control (on top of the text) to select the text. Type Years of Service to replace the default text.

8. Select all of the labels in the first column. Open the Format menu and point to the Align command. Click Left to align the new label on the left margin with the other labels.

9. Save the changes to the design of the form and switch to Form View. The new field appears in the form as shown in Figure 3-13. ◖▬▬ Each new field automatically becomes the last field in the Tab order. You will need to adjust the Tab order if users will be entering data into a field that you add to a form.

more

You can also add a bound field to a form in Design View. If you have forgotten a field that you need from one of your record sources you can easily add it to the form. First click the Field List button 🔲 on the Form Design toolbar to open the field list. All of the fields from the record sources for the form will be included in the field list. Drag a field name to the form. When you drag the field, the mouse pointer will turn into **⊥⊾⊦**. Position this field symbol where you want the upper-left corner of the text box to be positioned. When you release the mouse button, a text box for the field and a numbered label control will be added to the form. You will have to move, resize and edit the label appropriately just as you did in the Skill.

Figure 3-12 Adding an unbound text box to a form

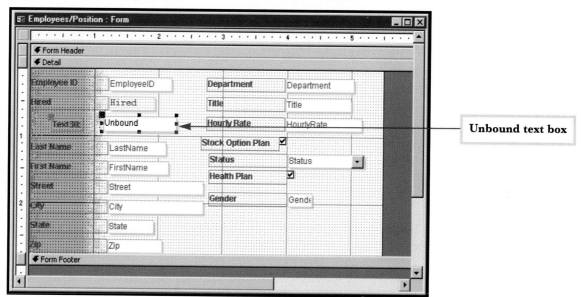

Figure 3-13 New Field in Form View

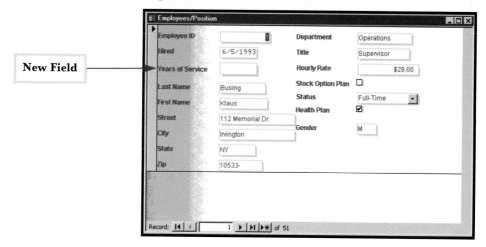

Practice

In the Tuning Tracker 2 database, open the Customers/Service Records form in Design View and add an unbound text box control directly below the Use text box. Move the new label control directly under the Use label. Use the Align Left command to line up all the labels. Drag the midpoint sizing handle on the right edge of the label control to the right until it reaches the Unbound text box. Drag the midpoint sizing handle on the bottom edge of the label downward to the 1¼ inch mark on the vertical ruler. Double-click the label control to select the text. Type Months Since Last Tuning to replace the default text. Save the changes, close the form, and minimize the application window.

skill | Using the Expression Builder

concept

You use the Expression Builder to help you create equations for calculated controls on a form or a report. Calculated text boxes are used to display the results of expressions. Expressions can use any of the Access functions you will find in the Expression builder, mathematical operators, raw values, and any field values on the form. Functions are predefined formulas that simplify the process of building equations. You can use these Access tools to display many useful calculations in a form such as the cost per unit of a particular product, or the number of years each employee has worked for a company.

do it!

Use the Expression Builder to build an equation that will calculate the number of years each employee has worked for the company and display the result in a new text box.

1. Open the Employee/Position form in Design View. Double-click the Unbound text box to open the property sheet.

2. Click the Data tab. Click in the Control Source property settings box. You use the Control Source property to specify what data appears in a control.

3. Click the Build button [...] that appears to the right of the Control Source property settings box after you select it. The Expression Builder opens.

4. Type: = since all Access expressions must begin with an equal sign.

5. Click the Common Expressions folder at the bottom of the left window in the lower half of the dialog box. Click Current Date in the middle window. Double-click Date() in the right window to add the current date function to the top window in the dialog box and begin the equation.

6. Click [-] (the minus sign operator) in the row of operator buttons just below the top window to add it to the equation.

7. Click the Employees/Position folder in the left window. Select the Hired text box in the field list that displays in the middle window. Click the Paste button [Paste] to add the value contained in the Hired field to the expression. The equation currently subtracts the date of hire from the current date to compute the number of days the employee has worked for the company. ◥◣ The text box is now a bound control. If you include a field value in the expression for a calculated control, the text box is bound to that field. The Years of Service field is bound to the Hired field because it must use the value in the Hired field to calculate the equation.

8. To calculate the number of years the employee has worked for the company, you must divide this equation by 365. First you must insert parenthesis around the equation so that the subtraction operation is performed first. Position the insertion point in front of Date. Click the opening parenthesis button [(].

9. Position the insertion point after the closing bracket on the Hired field. Click the closing parenthesis button [)].

10. Click the backslash button [/] to enter the division operator. Type: 365. The completed expression in the Expression Builder is shown in Figure 3-14.

(continued on AC 3.16)

Figure 3-14 The completed expression

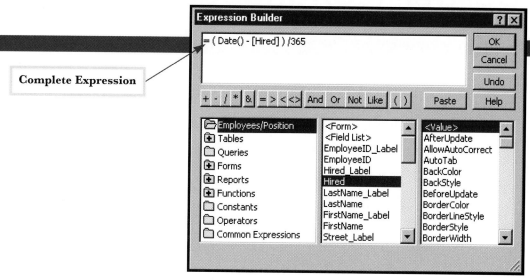

Complete Expression

Figure 3-15 The expression entered in the Control Source text box

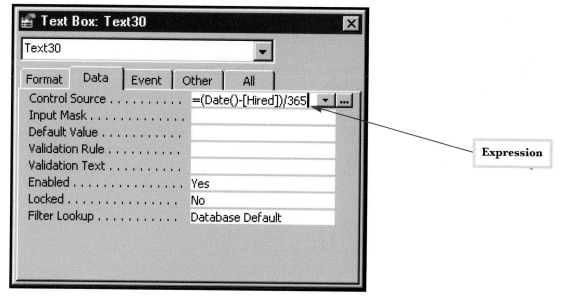

Expression

skill Using the Expression Builder (continued)

do it!

11. Click [OK] to close the Expression Builder. The equation has been entered in the Control Source property as shown in Figure 3-15 (see page AC 3.15). Click the Format tab on the property sheet.

12. Click in the Format property settings box. Click the list arrow and select Fixed on the drop-down list.

13. Click in the Decimal Places settings box. Click the list arrow and select 1 on the drop-down list. The Fixed decimal point settings on the Format tab are shown in Figure 3-16.

14. Click the Other tab. Set the Tab Stop property for the calculated control to No.

15. Close the property sheet. Close the Toolbox. Save the structural changes to the form.

16. Switch to Form View. Use the navigation buttons at the bottom of the form to view several records. The calculated control displays the number of years of service rounded to the nearest tenth. Close the form.

more

You must set the Tab Stop property for the Years of Service text box to No because users will not be entering or editing information in this field. The calculation will automatically update as the current date changes.

You can also simply type your equation in the text box control. For example, when you become comfortable with constructing equations without the help of the Expression Builder, you can simply type: =(Date()-[Hired])/365 in the text box control in Design View. Field names must be surrounded by square brackets. In Design View, you will see that the expression has replaced the word Unbound in the text box as shown in Figure 3-17.

Figure 3-16 **Format tab settings**

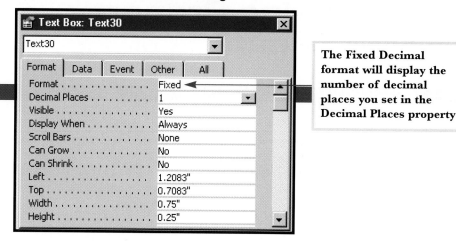

The Fixed Decimal format will display the number of decimal places you set in the Decimal Places property

Figure 3-17 **Expression entered in the text box in Design View**

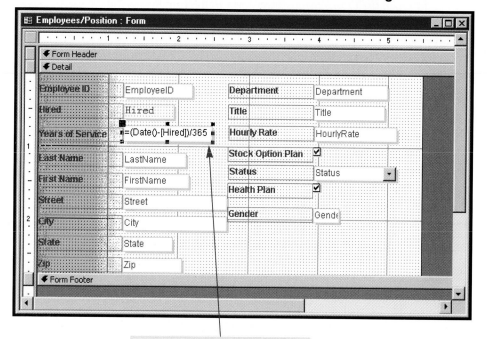

The length of the text box has been increased so that the entire equation is visible.

Practice

In the Tuning Tracker 2 database, open the Customers/Service Records form in Design View. Then, open the property sheet for the unbound text box. Click the Build button for the Control Source property. Use the Expression Builder to construct the equation that will calculate the months since the last tuning date, =(Date()-[Last Tuned])/30. Format the text box to round the answer to the nearest month (no decimal places). Save the change, view the calculations and close the form. Minimize the application window.

skill   Using Property Sheets

concept

You can also change properties for a control such as the font, font style, control size, border style, or special effects on the property sheet for that control. When you change the properties for a control using the Formatting toolbar, the new values are automatically entered on the property sheet. Generally, you use the property sheet only if a toolbar button or menu choice is not available on the Formatting toolbar.

do it!

Use the property sheets to format several controls on the form.

1. Open the Employee/Position form in the Employees 2 database in Design View.

2. Double-click the Last Name text box to open its property sheet.

3. Click the Format tab on the property sheet if necessary. Use the scroll bar to scroll down the list and locate the Font Size and Font Weight properties. Change the Font Size property to 10. Change the Font Weight property to Semi-Bold as shown in Figure 3-18.

4. Click the list arrow on the Object list box at the top of the property sheet. Select FirstName on the drop-down list. Apply the same two formatting changes.

5. Click the list arrow on the Object box and select Text 30 on the drop-down list. Locate the Fore Color property. Click in the settings box. Click the Build button [...], as shown in Figure 3-19.

6. Select the fifth square in the fifth row of the color palette as shown in Figure 3-20, to apply the same blue color to the text in the calculated control, and click [OK]. Change the Border Width property to 2pt to match the rest of the controls on the form.

7. Close the property sheet. Select the Department label. Press [Shift] and select all of the labels in that column. Click the Properties button [icon]. A Multiple selection property sheet opens.

8. Locate the Left property. Double click .7917 to highlight it. Type: 83 to enter 2.83 as shown in Figure 3-21. This will move the column of labels slightly to the right so that there is no overlap between the Street text box and the Health Plan label. Close the Multiple selection property sheet.

9. Save the changes. Switch to Form View to view the formatting changes. Close the form.

more

Using the property sheets to format your form is most useful when you must change minute details such as the spacing between controls. You can use the Left and Top properties to move controls to exact locations on the form. The Width and Height properties can be used to resize controls to your exact specifications. You can use the Border Style property to apply borders with dots or dashes in various styles. The Back Style property can be changed to transparent to make the background color for the form show through the control. If you try to close the form without saving the formatting changes, you will be prompted to save the changes to the design of the form.

Figure 3-18 Changing the Font Weight property

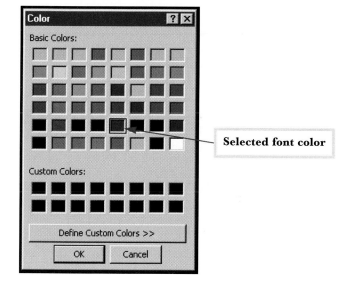

Changing the Font Weight property to Semi-bold

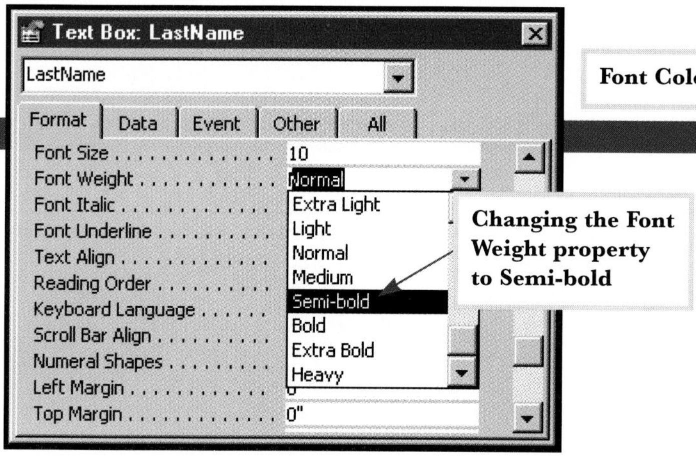

Figure 3-19 Changing the Fore Color property

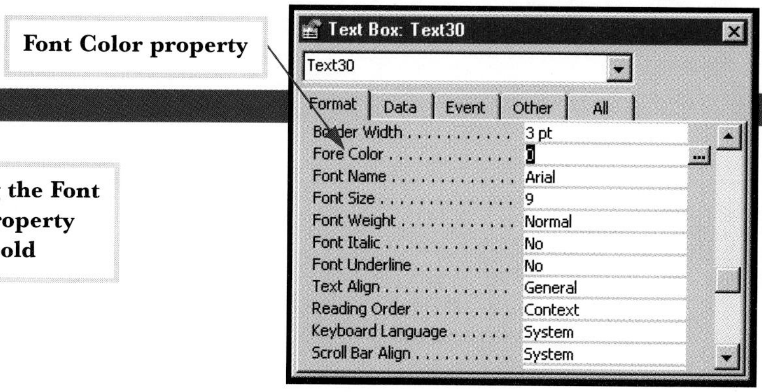

Font Color property

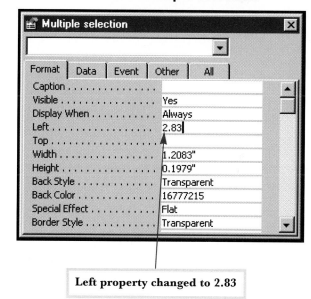

Figure 3-20 Selecting the font color

Selected font color

Figure 3-21 Changing the Left property for a multiple selection

Left property changed to 2.83

Practice

Open the Customers/Service Records form in the Tuning Tracker 2 database in Design View. Format the Piano Make field so that it is Semi-bold instead of Bold. Change the Tab Stop property for the calculated control so that it is not included in the tab order and apply a 2 pt border and the Shadowed Special Effect. Close the property sheet. Select all the labels in the second column and set their Left property to 2.95. Close the multiple selection property sheet. Select the first five text boxes in the second column. Set their Left property to 3.7. Save the changes, close the form, and minimize the application window.

skill
Entering Records Using a Form

concept

The purpose of a form is to simplify data entry and editing. The one-record-per-screen format is particularly useful for locating, entering, and editing records in the underlying record source. When you add a new record using the form, it is automatically added to the table or query to which the fields are bound. When you edit a record, the record sources are automatically updated.

do it!

Several new employees have been hired and the Employees database must be updated. Use the Employee/Position form to update the two tables.

1. Open the Employees/Position form in Form View. Click the New Record button ▶* on the Form View toolbar or the New Record navigation button ▶* at the bottom of the form.

2. Enter today's date in the Hired field. Press [Tab]. The Years of Service field is skipped because its Tab Stop property is set to No.

3. Type: Baker. Press [Tab]. Type: Alexander. Press [Tab]. Type: 347 Radford Dr. Press [Tab]. Type: Ardsley. Press [Tab]. The State field is skipped because it has a Tab Stop property of No.

4. Type: 10502. Press [Tab]. Type: Operations. Press [Tab]. Type: Data Entry Clerk. Press [Tab]. Type: 11.00. Press [Tab]. The Hourly Rate field is automatically formatted as Currency.

5. Press [Tab] to tab through the Stock Option Plan field. New employees are not eligible for the stock option plan until they have passed their six month anniversary. Press [Tab]. Select Full-Time on the drop-down list. Press [Tab]. Press [spacebar] to enter a check in the Health Plan check box. Press [Tab]. Type m. Press [Tab]. The M will be automatically capitalized as shown in Figure 3-22, but you will now see a blank record form.

6. Enter the record from Table 3-1.

7. Close the form. Click the Tables button on the Objects bar. Open the Employees table in Datasheet View and sort it in ascending order by the Employee ID field. Click the Last Record ▶| button. The two records have been added to the table as shown in Figure 3-23.

8. Close the table and the database without saving changes to the design of the table.

more

When you have many records to enter, creating a form and using it to enter your records is the most efficient method. The one-record-per screen format provides a clear working space for entering data and thus reduces data entry errors. If data must be entered into several tables in a relational database, a form that includes all of the pertinent fields will enable you to enter new records in one operation rather than having to open each table individually. In a table, you often have to scroll to locate a particular field in a record. When you create a form on the other hand, you can have all of the fields in one record display at one time. You can use the Find command to locate records and the Find and Replace dialog box to quickly edit text. You can also use the Filter by Selection button to locate records that meet certain criteria. For example, you can highlight the Zip Code field for record 1 and click the Filter by Selection button to locate all records of employees who live in the 10533 zip code area.

Figure 3-22 Entering a Record

Table 3-1 Record to be entered

Hired	3/31/01
Last Name	Farnsworth
First Name	Theresa
Street	982 Cisco Dr.
City	Eastchester
Zip Code	10709-
Department	Purchasing
Title	Account Manager
Hourly Rate	$20.00
Stock Option Plan	No
Status	Part-Time
Health Plan	Yes
Gender	f

Figure 3-23 New records are entered in the record source

Employees : Table

	Employee ID	Hired	Last Name	First Name	Street	City	State	Zip	Gend
+	34	1/2/98	Lau	Sydney	13 Forbes Rd	White Plains	NY	10601-	F
+	35	1/23/98	Alvarez	Alex	1111 Saxon Rd	White Plains	NY	10601-	M
+	36	2/7/98	Williamson	Lori	88 Smith Ln	White Plains	NY	10601-	F
+	37	4/21/98	Prakash	Dom	7 Garden Pl	Eastchester	NY	10709-	M
+	38	4/23/98	Adelman	Jody	123 Bell Rd	Hartsdale	NY	10530-	F
+	39	5/30/98	Borda	Ella	23 Broadway Ave	Scarsdale	NY	10583-	F
+	40	7/3/98	Lee	Mike	9 Livingston Pl	Eastchester	NY	10709-	M
+	41	8/1/98	Castle	Frank	51 Stone Ave	Elmsford	NY	10523-	M
+	42	9/6/98	Smith	Roberta	1 Cypress Ave	White Plains	NY	10601-	F
+	43	10/12/98	Martin	Edward	513 County Ridge Rd	Hartsdale	NY	10530-	M
+	44	12/8/98	Vukovich	Shelly	108 Smith Ave	White Plains	NY	10601-	F
+	45	12/15/98	DeBois	Kirby	25 Springfield Ln	Bronxville	NY	10708-	M
+	46	3/28/99	Watanabe	Tetsuo	99 Longfellow Dr	Rye	NY	10580-	M
+	47	3/28/99	McBride	Meghan	777 Pear Pl.	Irvington	NY	10533-	F
+	48	3/28/99	Greco	Hannah	12 Woodland Ave.	Irvington	NY	10533-	F
+	49	3/28/99	Caruso	Maria	131 Martin St	Scarsdale	NY	10583-	F
+	50	6/5/99	Geddes	Laura	1561 Tremont St.	Ardsley	NY	10502-	F
+	51	10/2/00	Trunk	James	45 Wolf Rd.	Croton	NY	10520-	M
+	52	8/5/01	Baker	Alexander	347 Radford Dr.	Ardsley	NY	10502-	M
+	53	3/31/01	Farnsworth	Theresa	982 Cisco Dr.	Eastchester	NY	10709-	F
*	(AutoNumber)						NY		

Two new records added to the table

Record: 53 of 53

Practice

Use the Start menu to open Microsoft Word. Then, open the Word file acprac3-8.doc and follow the instructions.

shortcuts

Function	Button/Mouse	Menu	Keyboard
Switch to Form View		In Form Design View, click View, then click Form View	[Alt]+[V], [F]
New Object: AutoForm		Click Insert, then click AutoForm,	[Alt]+[I], [O]
Show Toolbox/Hide Toolbox		In Form Design View, click View, then click Toolbox	[Alt]+[V], [X]
Properties (Open the property sheet)		In Form Design View, click View, then click Properties	[Alt]+[V], [P]
Show Field List/Hide Field List		In Form Design View, click View, then click Field List	[Alt]+[V], [L]

A. Identify Key Features

Identify the items indicated by callouts in Figure 3-24.

Figure 3-24 Microsoft Access window

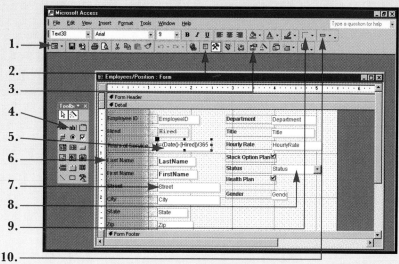

1.
2.
3.
4.
5.
6.
7.
8.
9.
10.

B. Select the Best Answer

11. This is used if you want to change the layout, choose a background template, or choose fields from several different tables when you create a form

    a. Formatting toolbar

12. This is used if you simply want to create a form that displays all the records from a, single table or query

    b. AutoForm

13. This is used to change many form characteristics such as the font, placement of text, and background color for a form

    c. Tab order

14. Property used to specify what data appears in a control—you can create a calculated control in any control that has this property

    d. Unbound

15. Refers to the order in which controls receive the focus when a user is pressing the Tab key to move through a form

    e. Property sheet

16. Property that is set to No so that the focus will skip the control on the form when the user is entering data

    f. Expression Builder

17. Control that is not linked to a record source

    g. Control Source

18. This is opened to add a bound field from a record source to a form

    h. Field List

19. This is used to help you create equations for calculated controls on a form

    i. Tab Stop

20. This is used to set the size and position for a control precisely and to change characteristics such as the border style and back style

    j. Form Wizard

quiz (continued)

C. Complete the Statement

21. When you use the Form Wizard you choose fields from:

   a. Only a single record source

   b. Only tables

   c. Multiple record sources

   d. A single table only

22. A bound control:

   a. Links to a field in an underlying database object

   b. Displays results of expressions that use functions and any field values on the form

   c. Is a predefined formula that simplifies the formula for building an equation

   d. Does not link to a record source

23. In Design View, you can enter an expression for a calculated control in all of the following ways except:

   a. Text box control where you want the result to display

   b. Expression Builder for the Control Source property for the control

   c. Label control for the corresponding text box

   d. Control Source property settings box for the control

24. You can create a columnar AutoForm using all of the following methods except:

   a. Select a record source in the Database window, open the Insert menu, and select the AutoForm command

   b. With Forms selected on the Objects bar, click Open on the Database window

   c. With Forms selected on the Objects bar, click New on the Database window toolbar and select AutoForm: Columnar in the New Form dialog box

   d. Click the list arrow on the New Object button on the Database toolbar and select the AutoForm command

25. The Auto Order button in the Tab Order dialog box will set the tab order so that the focus moves:

   a. According to the order of the fields in the record source

   b. Across the first line, down to the second line, and continuing left to right again

   c. According to the order in which the fields were added to the form

   d. Down the first column of fields and then down the second column

26. This type of control generally contains data from an underlying table or query.

   a. Bound control

   b. Unbound control

   c. Calculated control

   d. Text box control

27. This type of control is generally an identifier that tells the user what data to enter where.

   a. Bound control

   b. Unbound control

   c. Calculated control

   d. Text box control

28. The most common unbound control is a:

   a. text box

   b. checkbox

   c. label

   d. combo box

interactivity

Build Your Skills

1. Create and reformat an AutoForm. Enter a record using the form.

a. Open the Home Video Collection database. Click Forms on the Objects bar. Open the New Form dialog box. Create a columnar AutoForm using the Home Video Collection table.

b. Switch to Design View. Select both the VideoID text box and the GenreID text box. Open the Multiple selection property sheet and set the Width property to .3 to decrease the side of the controls Set the Width property for the Rating combo box to .7.

c. Select the Title text box. Drag the midpoint sizing handle on the right end of the text box to the 3-inch mark on the horizontal ruler. Switch to Form View. Use the navigation buttons to scroll through the records in the form. Return to Form Design View and increase the size of the text box to fit the longest title.

d. Change the font color in all of the text boxes to dark blue. Underline all of the labels. Save the changes. Name the form Home Video Collection.

e. Enter the following record using the form. Then close the form and the database.

Title	Genre ID	Genre	Rating	Comment	Star
Life Is Beautiful	3	Drama	PG-13	Excellent	Benigni, Braschi

2. Use the Form Wizard, modify a form, and set tab order.

a. Open the Office Furniture Inc database. Use the Form Wizard to create a form for entering new products into the Products table. Use the Justified layout and the Sumi Painting style. Leave the name for the form Products and open it in Design View.

b. Move the Units in Stock and Units on Order fields (both the text boxes and the labels) to the bottom row. Move the Unit Price field up to the end of the top row. Move the Units in Stock and Units on Order fields over to the left margin aligned with the Product ID field (see Figure 3-25, below).

c. Open the Tab Order dialog box and use the Auto Order button to set the tab order from left to right, top to bottom.

d. Save the changes, switch to Form View, and test the tab order.

Figure 3-25 Products form

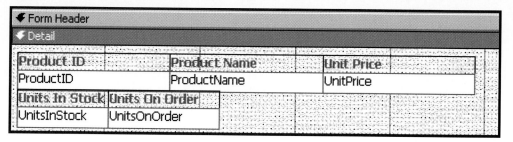

Access 2002

interactivity (continued)

Build Your Skills (continued)

3. Add a field to a form and use the Expression builder to construct a calculated control.

a. In the Office Furniture Inc database, open the Products form in Design View. Open the Toolbox. Add an unbound text box to the form to the right of the Units on Order field.

b. Use the move handles to position the text box and label in the justified layout to the right of the Units on Order field.

c. Select the new label control. Position the mouse pointer over the text until you have an I-beam pointer. Drag across the default text to select it. Type: Value in Inventory. The label size will automatically increase to fit the text that you type.

d. Double-click the Unbound text box to open the property sheet. Click the Data tab. Open the Expression Builder for the appropriate property.

e. Type: =. Remember, all expressions must begin with an equal sign. Create the expression that will calculate the inventory value of each product: =[UnitsInStock]*[UnitPrice].

f. On the Format tab, set the Format property to display the field as Currency. Format the new label with a Solid Border Style. Close the property sheet and save the changes.

g. Switch to Form View and use the navigation buttons to view the new calculated control. Is the calculated control a bound or an unbound control?

h. Return to Form Design View and resize and move any controls as necessary. Save the changes. Close the form and the database.

4. Use the Form Wizard, rearrange fields, set a new tab order, set properties using the property sheets, and create a calculated control.

a. Open the Address Book database. Use the Form Wizard to create a form using all the fields from both the Address and Contact Details tables. Be sure not to duplicate the shared field. Use the columnar layout and the Sumi Painting style. Keep the default name for the form (Addresses) and choose to modify the form's design.

b. In Design View, move the Relationship field one dot underneath the Birthday field so that it is the final field in the form. Move the Relationship field to last in the tab order to match the structural change you made to the form.

c. Move the TimesCalledPerMonth field up so that it is one dot below the Gender field. Move the TimesCalledPerMonth combo box directly underneath its label and increase the width of the label to the 1¾ inch mark on the horizontal ruler.

d. Add an unbound text box to the form underneath the Relationship combo box at the 4 inch mark on the horizontal ruler. Position the new controls one dot below the Relationship field and align the left edges of the labels in the second column of the form. Enter: Days Until B-Day in the Caption property for the new label control. Increase the width of the Days Until B-Day label to the 4 inch mark on the horizontal ruler.

e. Using the Expression Builder, construct an equation to calculate the number of days until the birthday for each Address Book entry {=[Birthday]-Date()}. Remember that you create a calculated control in the Control Source property and that all Access expressions must begin with an equal sign.

f. Change the correct property so that the Tab order will not include the calculated control. Save the changes.

g. Switch to Form View. Scroll through the records to view the new calculated control. Birthdays that have already passed in this calendar year must be entered for next year in order to calculate the number of days until the person's next birthday. Otherwise the formula will calculate the number of days since the birthday occurred, a negative value. Edit your data accordingly.

h. Return to Form Design View and resize the controls as necessary. Increase the width of the Birthday text box to the 6 inch mark on the horizontal ruler. Save the change. View the change in Form View, close the form and the database.

interactivity (continued)

Problem Solving Exercises

1. Open the Magazine Preferences database. Use the Form Wizard to create a form to enter data into the two tables with the one-to-one relationship. Be sure not to duplicate the shared field. Use the Columnar layout and any style you choose. Name the Form Magazine Subscribers.

2. View the form in Form View. Scroll through the records. Switch to Form Design View and resize the controls appropriately.

3. Change the typeface in one of the text boxes to Calisto MT in a 10 pt size. Change the Font color in the ID # text box to dark blue. Change the Font style to Bold.

4. Change the Font weight for the Last Name text box to Semi-bold. Save the structural changes to the form.

5. Since data entry personnel will not have to enter or edit data in the ID # field, set the Tab Stop property for the ID # text box to No. Save the changes.

6. Rearrange the order of the fields by moving fields on the form. Adjust the Tab Order accordingly. Save the change.

7. Use the property sheet to experiment with different border styles, border widths and border colors on one of the text box controls. When you are satisfied with the result save the change.

8. Use the form to add three more records to the tables. Close the database and Access.

Creating Reports

As you have learned, reports are the database objects that are specifically designed for printing. A report is a summary of the data contained in one or more tables or queries that can include calculations, graphics, and customized headers and footers. A report will often provide answers about the information in your database such as the yearly sales for a specific product or the payroll data for a particular week or month. When you create an Access report you can include calculations that are not included in other database objects. You can also include headers and footers to print identifying information at the top and bottom of every page. You can group and sort data to organize information efficiently and apply formatting effects to make your report both more attractive and easier to read and understand.

skills

§ **Creating an AutoReport**

§ **Using the Report Wizard**

§ **Formatting a Report**

§ **Adding a Calculated Control to a Report**

§ **Using a Query to Create a Report**

§ **Previewing and Printing a Report**

§ **Creating Mailing Labels**

Just like forms, reports can be created using a variety of methods. The AutoReport Wizards create a simple report containing the fields from a single record source. A columnar AutoReport is organized with each field on a separate line and the label for the field on the left. A tabular AutoReport is organized with each record on a single line and each of the field labels at the top of the page.

The Report Wizard will guide you through a series of dialog boxes which will enable you to choose the kind of report you wish to create. You can choose fields from multiple record sources and apply sorting and grouping options. The Label Wizard will create a report that is automatically formatted for printing mailing labels. After you have created any report you can modify its design in the Design View window.

When you have finished customizing your report you can preview it in either Print Preview or Layout Preview. Print Preview displays the report exactly as it will look when printed. Layout Preview displays the report with only a few sample rows of data to give you an idea of how the report will look without having to view every detail in the report.

Lesson Goal:

Create a report with an AutoReport Wizard. Use the Report Wizard to create a grouped report and the Label Wizard to create mailing labels. Customize reports, add calculated controls to a report, and preview and print a report.

skill | Creating an AutoReport

concept

You can create a standard report based on a single table or query using one of the AutoReport Wizards. An AutoReport can use either a columnar or a tabular layout. Just like AutoForm, AutoReport is the easiest and quickest way to create this type of database object, but it offers the most limited options. The AutoReport Wizard will arrange and format the data in the selected record source as an appealing report, which you can customize as necessary before printing.

do it!

Create an AutoReport in the Employees 2 database.

1. Start Access and open the Employees 2 database. Click Reports on the Objects bar to display the options for creating a report in the objects list.

2. Click [New] on the Database window toolbar to open the New Report dialog box.

3. Click AutoReport: Tabular. Click the list arrow on the Choose the table or query where the object's data comes from list box.

4. Click Employees on the drop-down list as shown in Figure 4-1 to select the Employees table as the record source. Click [OK].

5. A standard tabular report is created using all of the fields in the Employees table. The report is opened in Print Preview. Use the navigation buttons at the bottom of the Print Preview window and the scroll bars to preview the three pages of the report. As you can see the output from an AutoReport is only slightly better than a printout from a datasheet (tabular) or a form (columnar). To create more appealing and useful reports you should use the Report Wizard.

6. Click [ ] to switch to Design View. Click the AutoFormat button [ ] on the Report Design toolbar to open the AutoFormat dialog box. Leave the Corporate style for the report selected and click [OK].

7. Practice resizing and moving the labels in the Page Header section of the report and the text boxes in the Detail section of the report to create more space between the columns in the report as shown in Figure 4-2.

8. Close the report without saving it.

more

You can also open the New Report dialog box by clicking the list arrow on the New Object button on the Database toolbar. Select Report on the drop-down menu. The New Object button displays the last object you created. If the last object you created was an AutoReport the New Object: AutoReport button [ ] displays.

You can also create a simple columnar AutoReport based on a record source you select in the Database window. For example, with Queries selected on the Objects bar, you can select the Gross Weekly Pay query in the Database window. Then you can either open the Insert menu and select the AutoReport command or click the list arrow on the New Object button and select AutoReport. Access creates the report using the last autoformat you used. If you have not previously created a report with a wizard or used the AutoFormat command, the Standard AutoFormat is used. Reports created using this method do not include report headers or footers or page headers or footers.

Figure 4-1 New Report dialog box

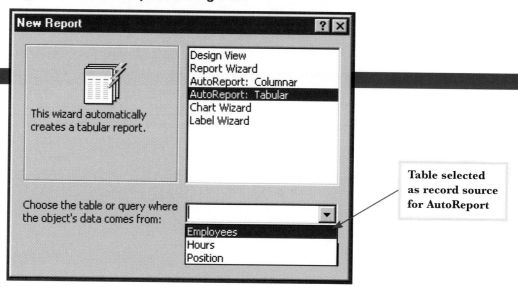

Table selected as record source for AutoReport

Figure 4-2 Employees AutoReport with the Corporate AutoFormat applied

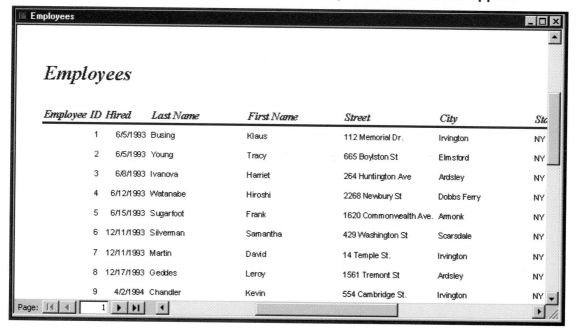

Access 2002

Practice

Open another Access application window and the Recipes database. Create a tabular AutoReport using the Quick Recipes query. Do not save it. Leave the application window and Recipes database open for subsequent Practice sessions. Minimize the application window.

skill   Using the Report Wizard

concept

When you create a report with the Report Wizard, you can select fields from more than one record source, determine the style for the report as it is being created, choose from among several different layout designs, and decide how you want the records in the report to be grouped and sorted. When you group a report based on a field each group is a separate section in the report. For example, you can group employees by Department so that managers will be able to easily skim a report to locate the information for their department.

do it!

Use the Report Wizard to create an Employees report.

1. Click the Reports button on the Objects bar in the Employees 2 Database window. Double-click Create report by using wizard. The first Report Wizard dialog box opens.

2. With Table: Employees selected in the Tables/Queries list box, click the Select All Fields >> button to move all of the fields from the Available Fields scrolling list box to the Selected Fields box.

3. Use the Remove Field < button to remove the Employee ID, Hired and Gender fields as shown in Figure 4-3. ◀◀◀ Another way to move a field from the Available Fields box to the Selected Fields box or vice versa is to double-click it. No matter which side the field is on, when you double-click it, it will move to the opposite side.

4. Click the list arrow on the Tables/Queries list box. Select Table: Position on the drop-down list.

5. Select the First Name field in the Selected Fields box. Access will add the new fields from the Positions table after the field you select in the Selected Fields box.

6. Use the Add Field > button to add the Department and Title fields to the Selected Fields box as shown in Figure 4-4. Click Next >.

7. Select the Department field in the box underneath the question; Do you want any grouping levels? Click >. The fields in the report will be grouped by Department as shown in Figure 4-5. Click Next >.

8. Click the list arrow on the first sort order list box. Select Last Name on the drop-down list.

9. Click the list arrow on the second sort order list box. Select First Name on the drop-down list. The records will first be sorted by last name. In cases where there are identical last names, First Name will serve as the secondary sort field. Click Next >. ◀◀◀ By default, Access will sort the fields in ascending order. To switch to a descending sort, click the Ascending button to change the button caption to Descending.

10. Leave the layout in the Stepped format and click the Landscape option button in the Orientation section. Click Next >. ◀◀◀ If you do not choose any grouping levels for a report, your layout choices will be limited to three: Columnar, Tabular, or Justified. The layouts in Step #10 are only available for grouped reports.

(continued on AC 4.6)

Figure 4-3 Removing fields from a report

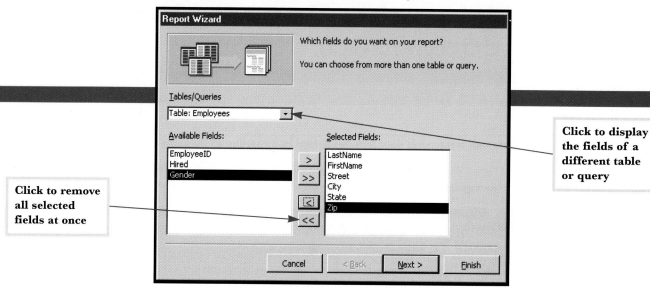

Click to display the fields of a different table or query

Click to remove all selected fields at once

Figure 4-4 Adding fields from a second record source

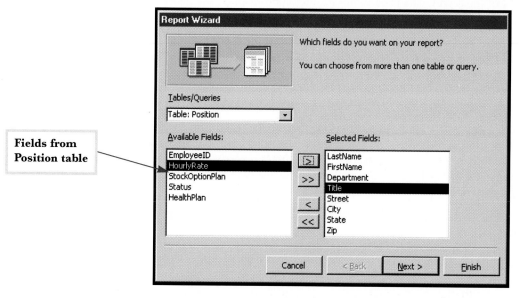

Fields from Position table

Figure 4-5 Adding a grouping level to a report

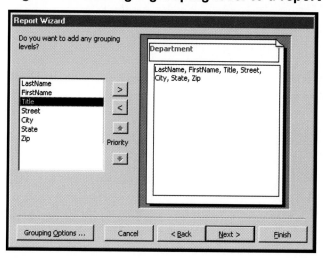

skill | Using the Report Wizard (continued)

do it!

11. Choose the Corporate style and click [Next >].

12. Leave the name for the report Employees and click [Finish] to open the report in Print Preview as shown in Figure 4-6. Increase the size of the window as necessary.

13. Click the list arrow on the Zoom list box. Select 75% on the drop-down list. The onscreen magnification is decreased allowing you to see more of the report.

14. Click the Multiple Pages button [▦] on the Print Preview toolbar. Drag across the top row on the drop-down palette to select the 1x3 display and click the left mouse button to display all three pages of the report.

15. Use the magnification glass pointer to click the lower left hand corner of the second page of the report. The page footer for the report displays the date in the left hand corner of each page and the page number out of how many total pages in the report in the right-hand corner of each page. Click the magnification glass pointer again to zoom out.

16. Click the One Page button [▣] on the Print Preview toolbar. Close the report.

more

The report header which prints once at the beginning of the report contains the title for the report. The page header prints at the top of every page and contains the labels or column headings. When you group records, the Report Wizard automatically creates a group header which contains the name for the like field that defines each group. You can add a group footer, as you will see in the next two skills, to include summary information about the group such as a count, sum or average.

Print Preview displays reports as they will appear when printed. As you saw in the exercise, you can change the onscreen magnification percentage in the Zoom list box either by selecting a different percentage on the drop-down list or by typing in the magnification percentage you want. Changing the magnification does not change the size at which the document is printed. The Fit setting adjusts the magnification of the page to fit the size of the window. You can switch between the magnification you selected and Fit using the magnification glass pointer or the Zoom button [🔍] on the Print Preview toolbar.

Figure 4-6 Employees report grouped by Department

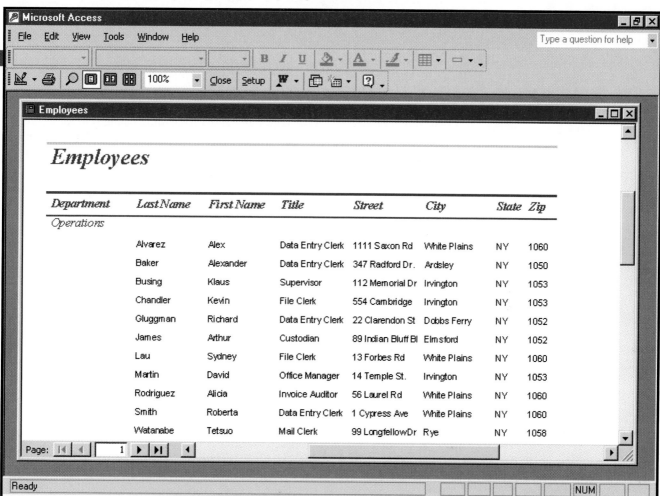

Practice

Fill in all of the Which Meal? fields in the Recipes table. Use the Report Wizard to create a report containing the Recipe Name, Food Category, Which Meal? Time to Prepare, and Number of Servings fields. Choose to view the data by Food Category. Add a grouping level for Which Meal? Click the Raise Priority button to make it the primary grouping field. Use the Outline 2 layout and the Corporate style. Keep the default name.

 Formatting a Report

concept

Just as in a form, all of the objects in a report can be modified in Design View. You can change the organization or layout of your report and apply formatting changes to the entire report or to individual sections. You can rearrange and resize fields, add special effects, align and format text, and add color. In a grouping report you can also add group footers and set group properties to improve the appearance of your report.

do it!

Apply formatting effects and add a group footer to the Employees report.

1. Select the Employees report in the Employees 2 database window. Click ⟨Design⟩ on the Database window toolbar to open the report in Design View.

2. Select the label control with the report title in the Report Header section of the report. Click the Underline button ⟨U⟩ on the Formatting (Form/Report) toolbar.

3. Click in the vertical ruler to the left of the Department label in the Page Header section of the report to select all of the label controls in the page header. Increase the font size for the controls to 12 pt.

4. Select the Department text box in the Department (group) Header section. Make the text bold and underlined.

5. Select the Last Name text box in the Detail section of the report. Make the text bold and change the font color to the medium blue color (the third row, sixth square) on the Font/Fore Color palette.

6. Select the text box containing the Now function (=Now()) in the Page Footer section of the report. Decrease the size of the text box and change the background color for the text box to light blue (the last row, fifth square on the Fill/Back Color palette).

7. Click the Sorting and Grouping button ⟨≣⟩ on the Report Design toolbar.

8. Click in the Group Footer settings box in the Group Properties section at the bottom of the dialog box. Click the list arrow and select Yes on the drop-down list to add a group footer to the report.

9. Click in the Keep Together property settings box. Click the list arrow and select Whole Group. Check your settings against Figure 4-7.

10. Close the Sorting and Grouping dialog box. Save the changes and click ⟨🔍⟩ to switch to Print Preview. Use the navigation buttons to view the formatting changes (see Figure 4-8).

more

To access the property sheet for the entire report (Figure 4-9), double-click the small gray box ⬜ in the upper-left corner of the report window at the intersection of the vertical and horizontal rulers. This is called the Report Selector icon. When the form is selected, the Report Selector icon will contain a black square ⬛.

Each section of the report also has a property sheet. To the left of each section bar is a small gray box on the vertical ruler. These are the Section Selectors. Double-click a Section Selector to open the property sheet for the section.

If you have the appropriate data you can group a report by more than one level, creating a report that resembles an outline, with subgroups nested within the primary group. The Group On property is used to instruct Access when to begin a new group of records. The default Each Value setting tells the program to group identical values. You can use the Interval setting to organize your report based on a range of entries. For example, if you group a number data type field using an interval of 25, Access will group records with the values, 0 to 24, 25 to 49, 50 to 99, and 100 to 124 and so on.

The With First Detail setting for the Keep Together property instructs Access to print all of the data from the group header through the Detail section for the first entry in the group on the same page. It ensures that a group header will not print at the bottom of a page with no records underneath it.

Figure 4-7 Sorting and Grouping dialog box

Sorting and Grouping symbol indicates that Access uses the field or expression to group the records

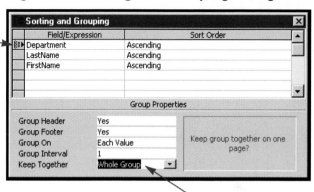

Figure 4-8 Formatted Employees report

Whole Group setting ensures that the entire group will be kept together on one page of the report

Figure 4-9 Property sheet of the Entire Report

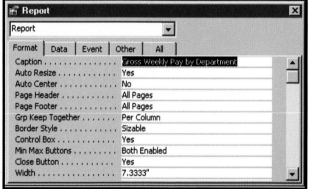

Practice

In the Recipes database, open the Recipes report in Design View. Open the Sorting and Grouping dialog box and set the Keep Together property to Whole Group. Format the Which Meal text box so that the entries display in an 11 pt Tahoma font in royal blue. Drag the right midpoint sizing handle on the Which Meal? label to the 1¼ inch mark on the horizontal ruler to decrease the label size. Move the Which Meal? text box to the left so that it is two dots to the right of the label. Save the changes and close the report.

skill

Adding a Calculated Control to a Report

 MOUS Skill

concept

You can add fields to a report by adding unbound text box controls just as you did in the form. You can also use the Expression Builder to create an equation to calculate a value that you want to include in the report. Calculated controls are often quite useful in a report. You can calculate the quantity on hand of a certain product times its unit price to determine the value of your inventory, or you can use the Sum, Average or Count functions to summarize data for each group of records in a report.

do it!

Add unbound text boxes to the Group Footer and Report Footer sections of the report. Use the Count function to calculate the number of entries in each group and the total number of employees listed in the report.

1. Open the Employees report in the Employees 2 database in Design View.

2. Click the Toolbox button ⚒ on the Report Design toolbar. Click the Text Box button **abl** to activate the Text Box pointer.

3. Click at the left edge of the Department Footer section. Use the move handles to position the new unbound text box and label control.

4. Click the label to select it. Drag to select the default numbered text in the label control. Type: Count.

5. Double-click the text box to open its property sheet. Click the Data tab. Type: =Count([Department]) in the Control Source property settings box. Close the property sheet. ◥ Remember, all formulas must begin with an equals sign and all field names must be enclosed in brackets. Parentheses must surround the expression on which a function is being performed.

6. Position the mouse pointer on the bottom edge of the Report Footer section bar until it turns into a vertical resizing pointer. Drag downward to create a section just large enough for a calculated control.

7. Click **abl** in the Toolbox. Click once at the left edge of the Report Footer section to insert an unbound text box and label. Use the move handles to reposition the two controls. Close the Toolbox. Replace the default label text with: Grand Count.

8. Click the calculated control in the Group Footer section to select it. Drag to select the expression in the text box. Click the Copy button 📋 on the Report Design toolbar.

9. Click the unbound text box in the Report Footer section to select it. Click the control again to enter text. Click the Paste button 📋 to enter the formula. The Report Design window is shown in Figure 4-10.

10. Save the changes to the report and switch to Print Preview. Click the Last Page button ▶| . The last page of the report is shown in Figure 4-11. The expression using the Count function has totaled the number of records in each group and the number of records in the report.

11. Close the report, saving the changes if necessary.

more When you are entering a lengthy expression in the Control Source property for a report control, you can either right-click the settings box and click Zoom on the shortcut menu or use the keyboard combination [Shift]+[F2] to open the Zoom dialog box. The Zoom dialog box will enable you to see the entire equation as you are entering it.

The report footer is printed after the last group and appears only once, at the end of the report. The page footer is always the last section to print at the bottom of each page.

Figure 4-10 Calculated controls added to the group and report footers

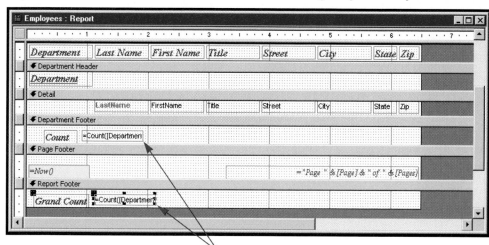

The same expression counts the numbers of records in each group in the group footers and the total number of records in the report in the report footer

Figure 4-11 Calculations in the report

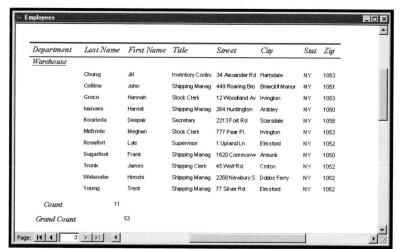

Practice

Add an unbound text box to the report footer. Create a calculated control to count the total number of recipes in the database. Format the calculated text box in an 11 pt. Times New Roman font in dark blue to match the report. Enter Total Recipes as the label text. Create a light gray, sunken, 2 pt. border around both controls. Save the changes and close the report.

skill   Using a Query to Create a Report

concept

Although you can select fields from different tables and queries in the first step of the Report Wizard, you may find it easier to create a query to consolidate the fields that you want first. This will simplify the process if you decide to add fields or criteria later. You can easily add fields to the underlying query to add them to the field list for the report. You can also change criteria in the Query design grid to expand or limit the number of records displayed in the report.

do it!

Create a report based on a query including a summary of the records for each department.

1. In the Employees 2 database, click Queries on the Objects bar. Create a query with the Simple Query Wizard. From the necessary record sources, include (in order) the EmployeeID, LastName, FirstName, Department, Title, WeekEnding and Gross Weekly Pay fields as shown in Figure 4-12.

2. Make the query a detail query, and name it Gross Pay Report Query. Close the query.

3. Click Reports on the Objects bar. Double-click Create a report by using wizard to begin the Report Wizard. Add all of the fields in the Gross Pay Report Query except Week Ending to the Selected Fields box. Click Next > .

4. Group the report based on the Department field. Click Next > .

5. Sort the report in Ascending order based on the Last Name and First Name fields. Click Summary Options ... .

6. Click the Sum checkbox in the Summary Options dialog box as shown in Figure 4-13 to instruct Access to calculate the sum of the gross weekly pay field for each department. Leave the Detail and Summary radio button selected and click OK .
Click Next > .

7. Leave the report in the Stepped layout and Portrait orientation. Apply the Corporate style if necessary. Name the report Gross Weekly Pay by Department and open it in Design View.

8. Rearrange the Employee ID, Last Name, and First Name fields (both the text boxes and the labels) so that the Employee ID field is the first field after the Department grouping. To select adjacent controls you can also click and drag to create a rectangle around the controls you want to select. The Select Objects button �+ must be selected on the Toolbox.

9. Increase the size of the Employee ID label control. Select the report title and add 10/24/01 to the title. The changes to the report design are shown in Figure 4-14.

(continued on AC 4.14)

Figure 4-12 **Creating a record source for a report**

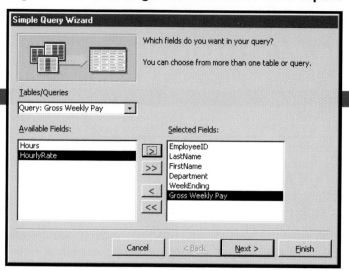

Figure 4-13 **Summary Options dialog box**

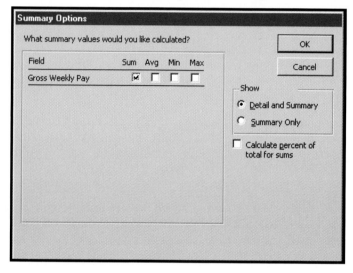

Figure 4-14 **Gross Weekly Pay 10/24/01 report in Design View**

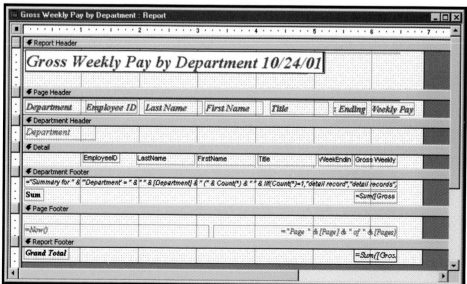

skill   Using a Query to Create a Report (continued)

do it!

10. Select the two calculated text boxes labeled Sum and Grand Total in the Department Footer and Report Footer sections and open the multiple selection property sheet. Set the Format property to Currency as shown in Figure 4-15 and close the property sheet. You can also right-click a selected control or group of controls and click Properties on the shortcut menu to open the property sheet.

11. Switch to Print Preview and use the scroll bars and the navigation buttons to view the report. A summary has been created for each group. The number of records and gross weekly pay total for each department display in the group footers. However, there are two weeks of pay displayed for each employee (see Figure 4-16). Save the changes to the report and close it.

12. Open the Gross Pay Report Query in Design View. In the Criteria cell for the Week Ending field, type =10/24/01. Press [Enter]. Save the change and close the query.

13. Open the Gross Weekly Pay by Department report in Print Preview. Changing the criteria in the underlying record source has eliminated the unwanted records in the report. Close the report.

14. Right-click the report name in the Database window. Click the Rename command. Position the insertion point at the end of the title and add: 10/24/01 to the report name. Press [Enter].

more

Creating a query to gather the fields you want for your report into one database object is a good practice. If you decide you want to add fields later, it is easier to add the fields to the underlying query. To add fields and criteria to the report itself you must either change the properties of the report or add unbound text box controls and create expressions to retrieve the desired value. It is much easier to create a query to select the fields and use it as the record source for the report.

Figure 4-15 Applying the Currency format to a multiple selection

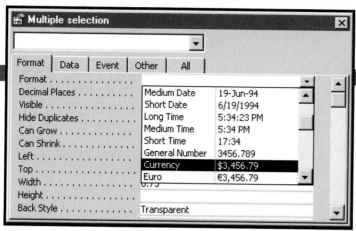

Figure 4-16 Completed report

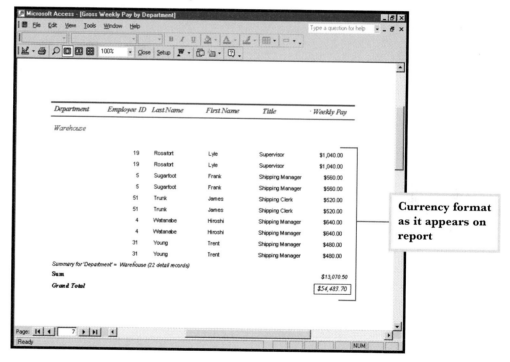

Currency format as it appears on report

Practice

Use the Simple Query Wizard to create a query containing the Which Meal, Recipe Name, Food Category, and Vegetarian fields. Name the query Vegetarian and enter Yes in the Criteria cell for the Vegetarian field in the Query design grid. Create a report with the Recipe Name, Food Category and Which Meal fields from the query grouped by Food Category. Use the Stepped layout, Corporate style, and name it Vegetarian.

skill

Previewing and Printing a Report

concept

Before you print a report you should make sure that all of the controls are correctly aligned. Misaligned controls in a report will be obvious and will detract from the effectiveness of the printed document. You can display just a few sample records in Layout view to check that the controls in every section of the report are properly displayed. Then you can adjust the margins, change the page orientation, or adjust the paper size if necessary in the Page Setup dialog box. Finally you can return to Print Preview and print the report.

do it!

Align the controls in the Gross Weekly Pay by Department 10/24/01 report, preview the report in Layout Preview, adjust the page margins, and print the report.

1. Open the Gross Weekly Pay by Department 10/24/01 report in the Employees 2 database in Design View.

2. Click in the vertical ruler to the left of the Department label in the Page Header section of the report to select all of the label controls in the section. Open the Format menu, highlight Align and click Top. The top edges of all of the controls are aligned with the uppermost selected label.

3. Click in the vertical ruler to the left of the Employee ID text box in the Detail section of the report. Open the Format menu, highlight Align, and click Bottom. There is now a straight line along the bottom edge of the five controls.

4. Click at the ¼ inch mark on the horizontal ruler to select all of the controls on the left edge of the report. Align the controls Left as shown in Figure 4-17.

5. Click at the 6 inch mark on the horizontal ruler to select the controls on the right edge of the report. Align the controls along the Right edge of the report.

6. Open the View menu and click the Layout Preview command. A sample report showing all of the controls but not all of the Detail section opens. You may still need to align some of the text boxes in the center of the report with their corresponding labels. If so, return to Design View, select the appropriate controls, and use the correct Align command to fix their placement on the report. Save the changes.

7. Open the File menu and click the Page Setup command. The Page Setup dialog box opens on the Margins tab.

8. Double-click in the Top text box to highlight the setting. Type .75 to set the margin to ¾ of an inch. Press [Tab]. Type: .75 to reset the Bottom margin, as shown in Figure 4-18.

9. Click the Page tab. If necessary you can change the page orientation or paper size on this page of the dialog box. Click ⟨ OK ⟩.

10. Return to Design View. Click 🔍.

11. Open the File menu and click the Print command. Click the Pages radio button in the Print Range section. Enter 1 in both the From and the To text box to print only the first page of the report. Click ⟨ OK ⟩ to print the page. Close the Print Preview window.

more   Access stores the page setup settings for forms and reports so you only have to set them once. For tables and queries, you must set the page setup options every time you print. The default margin settings (1 inch Top, Bottom, Left, and Right) can be changed on the General tab in the Options dialog box. You open the Options dialog box by clicking the Options command on the Tools menu. Changing the default margins will not affect the margin settings on existing forms and reports.

The Printer section in the Print dialog box tells Access which printer it is sending data to and where that printer is located. The Properties button opens the Printer Properties dialog box where you can change the paper size and page orientation, or adjust the print quality and color intensity.

Figure 4-17 Aligning controls

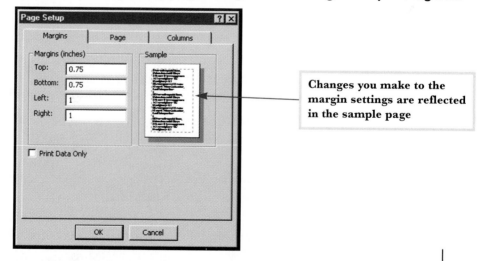

This aligns the left edge of each of the seven selected controls

Figure 4-18 Adjusting page margins in the Page Setup dialog box

Changes you make to the margin settings are reflected in the sample page

Practice

Open the Vegetarian Report in Design View. Use the Report Selector to select the report and click the AutoFormat button. Change the report style to Bold. Open the report in Layout Preview. Click the Two Pages button. Open the Page Setup dialog box and decrease the left and right margin to ½ inch. Close the report, saving the changes. Close the Recipes database.

skill | Creating Mailing Labels

concept

In an office many tasks involve bulk-mailings, for example, correspondence with employees, invoices to customers, and remittances to suppliers. The Label Wizard can be used to create mailing labels directly from a database. Mailing labels are a special type of multi-column report specifically designed to be printed on many different brands of adhesive labels.

do it!

Create mailing labels for the Employees 2 database.

1. With Reports selected on the Objects bar on the Employees 2 Database window click [New] on the Database window toolbar to open the New Report dialog box.

2. Click Label Wizard in the New Report dialog box. Choose the Employees table as the record source. Click [OK].

3. Drag the scroll bar down the list of Product numbers in the: What label size would you like? scrolling list box to locate the Avery USA 5095 label as shown in Figure 4-19. Click to select it and click [Next >]. If you cannot locate the correct label, click the English radio button in the Unit of Measure section and click the list arrow on the Filter by manufacturer list box and select Avery on the drop-down list.

4. Click the list arrow on the Font name list box and select Lucinda Handwriting on the drop-down list.

5. Click the list arrow on the Font weight list box and select Semi-bold on the drop-down list.

6. Click the list arrow on the Font size list box and select 10 on the drop-down list. Click [Next >].

7. Select First Name in the Available fields scrolling list box. Click the Add Field button [>]. Press the space bar and add the Last Name field. Press [Enter].

8. Select the Street field and click [>]. Press [Enter]. Double-click the City field to add it to the label. Type a comma (,), press the space bar, and double-click the State field to add it to the label.

9. Press the space bar. Double-click the Zip field to add it to the label. The prototype label is shown in Figure 4-20. Click [Next >].

10. Double-click the Last Name field in the Available fields list box. Double-click the First Name field to make it the secondary sorting criterion. Click [Next >].

11. Click [Finish] to accept the default name for the report and open it in Print Preview as shown in Figure 4-21. Close the report.

more

The Label Wizard includes the correct dimensions for numerous commercial adhesive labels made for dot-matrix or laser printers. After you select the label type, Access sets up the number of columns, rows per page and margins for the Detail section of the report. In the first wizard dialog box you can create your own custom label to accommodate labels with unusual sizes or for manufacturers that are listed in the dialog box.

Figure 4-19 Choosing the label type in the Label Wizard

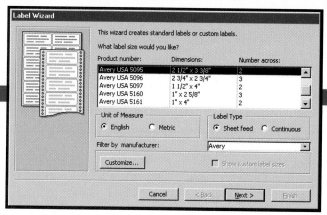

Figure 4-20 Prototype label

Select fields
for label here

Type your own fields
on the prototype here

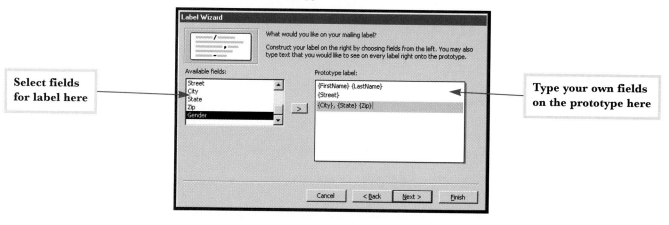

Figure 4-21 Labels in Print Preview

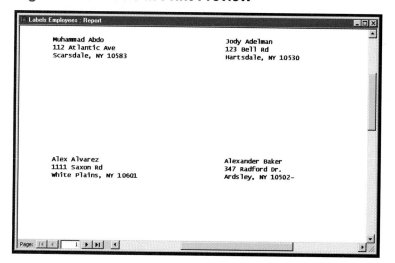

Access 2002

Practice

Open the Tuning Tracker 2 database. Use the Customers table to create mailing labels for the company. Use the Avery 5095 label and the Times New Roman font in an 11 pt size and a semi-bold weight. Create the prototype label with the correct punctuation and spacing. Sort the labels by last and first name. Close Access.

shortcuts

Function	Button/Mouse	Menu	Keyboard
Print Preview	🔍	In Report Design View: click View, then click Print Preview	[Alt]+[V], [V]
AutoFormat	📝	In Form or Report Design View: Click Format, then click AutoFormat	[Alt]+[O], [F]
New Object: AutoReport		On the Database toolbar: click Insert, then click AutoReport	[Alt]+[I], [E]
Show Sorting and Grouping/Hide Sorting and Grouping	≣	In Report Design View: click View, then click Sorting and Grouping	[Alt]+[V], [S]
One Page, Two Pages, Multiple Pages	▦	In Print Preview: click View, point to Pages, then click One, Two, Four, Eight or Twelve	[Alt]+[V], [A], ([O], [T], [F], [E], or [W])
Print	(to bypass the Print dialog box) 🖨	Click File, then click Print	[Alt]+[F], [P]
Zoom	🔍		

A. Identify Key Features

Name the first three items indicated by callouts and match the rest with the correct answer below.

Figure 4-22 A report in Design View

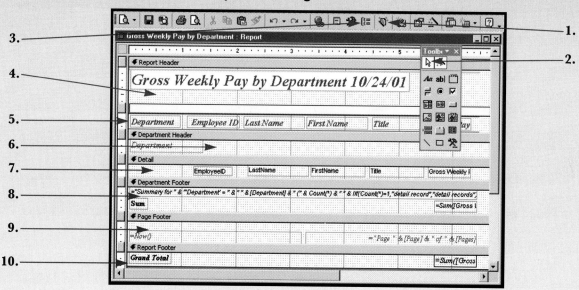

3.

4.

5.

6.

7.

8.

9.

10.

1.

2.

Access 2002

B. Select the Best Answer

11. Either prints an entire group from header to footer on the same page or prints all of the data from the group header through the first entry in the Detail section on the same page

12. Property you set to Currency to display calculated controls with a dollar sign and two decimal places

13. Used to create a standard report based on a single record source

14. Small gray box in the upper-left corner of the report window that is used to access the property sheet fo the entire report

15. Used to switch between a selected magnification percentage and a report sized to fit in the window

16. Used to create a special type of multicolumn report specifically designed to be printed on an adhesive label

17. Small gray box on the vertical ruler that you can use to open the property sheet of a report section

18. Dialog box found within the Report Wizard where you can set Access to calculate the sum, average, minimum value, or maximum value for each data set in a grouped report

19. Displays a report with only a few sample rows of data to give you an idea of how the report will look without having to view every detail

20. Contains commands for viewing one, two, or multiple pages of a repot

a. Summary Options

b. Section Selector

c. Label Wizard

d. Layout Preview

e. Format property

f. Keep Together property

g. Print Preview toolbar

h. Report Selector

i. Auto Report Wizard

j. Zoom

quiz (continued)

C. Complete the Statement

21. To group a report based on a selected field you must:

    a. Set the Group On property to Each Value in the Sorting and Grouping dialog box

    b. Set the Group Header, Group Footer or both properties to Yes on the property sheet for the field you want to group by

    c. Set the Group Header, Group Footer or both properties to Yes in the Grouping and Sorting dialog box

    d. Set the Grouping property to Yes on the property sheet for the field you want to group by

22. When you are entering a lengthy expression in the Control Source property for a report control, you can create a clearer working space to see the entire equation as you are entering it by: Pick two

    a. Opening the View menu and clicking the Zoom command

    b. Using the keyboard combination [Shift] + [F2] to open the Zoom dialog box

    c. Clicking the Zoom button on the Print Preview toolbar to open the Zoom dialog box

    d. Right-clicking the settings box and clicking Zoom on the shortcut menu

23. To select multiple controls on a report you can do all of the following except:

    a. Press the Shift key down and click each control you want to include.

    b. Click the Section selector for a section of the report in which you want to select all of the controls

    c. Click in the horizontal or vertical ruler above or to the left of the row or column of controls you want to select

    d. Make sure the Select Objects button is selected on the Toolbox and click and drag to create a rectangle around the controls you want to select

24. The Detail section of a report will usually contain this type of control

    a. Text box controls

    b. Label controls

    c. Calculated controls

    d. Combo box controls

25. A group footer will usually contain this type of control

    a. Text box controls

    b. Label controls

    c. Calculated controls

    d. Combo box controls

26. The page header will usually contain this type of control

    a. Text box controls

    b. Label controls

    c. Calculated controls

    d. Combo box controls

27. The correct expression for calculating the sum of the values in the Extended Price field is:

    a. Sum([ExtendedPrice])

    b. = Sum[ExtendedPrice]

    c. =Sum({ExtendedPrice})

    d. =Sum([ExtendedPrice])

28. You can use this function to insert the current system date and time in a field

    a. Date()

    b. Time()

    c. Now()

    d. Date/Time()

interactivity

Build Your Skills

1. Use the Report Wizard to create a grouped report. Add a group footer and calculated controls and customize the report.

   a. Open the Home Video Collection database. Use the Report Wizard to create an Inventory report grouped by Rating. Include the Title, Genre, Rating, Comment, and Star, fields. Sort the report in ascending order alphabetically by Title within each group. Use the Outline 1 format in portrait orientation in any style you choose. Name the Report Home Video Inventory.

   b. Open the Report in Design View. Add a group footer to the report and program Access to keep each group together on the same page.

   c. Add an unbound text box to the group footer. Enter the expression that will count the number of videos in each rating group. Also add a calculated control to the report footer to count the total number of videos in the inventory. Enter appropriate label text for each calculated control. Switch to Layout Preview.

   d. Align the calculated controls and format the text boxes so that they display with a semi-bold font style and are enclosed in a 3 pt. gray border with a shadowed effect.

   e. View the complete report in Print Preview and move and resize any fields as necessary. If the style you have chosen has any lines separating the labels in the group header from the Detail section, select the line controls and increase their lengths as necessary. Align the controls as necessary.

   f. Save the changes and close the report.

2. Create a query to serve as the record source for a report. Use the Report Wizard to create a report including group and report summaries and totals. Format the report and change the criteria in the record source to remove records from the report.

   a. Open the Office Furniture database. Use the Simple Query Wizard to generate a detail query that includes (in order) the Order ID, Order Date, Company Name, Units Ordered, Product Name, and Unit Price fields. Name the query Orders Query and open it in Design View.

   b. Create a calculated field in the Query design grid named Invoice Total. Create the expression that will calculate the result. Note: In the real world this would be a more complex calculation including the tax, shipping, and any discounts applied to the order. For now just create the simple expression.

   c. Save the changes to the query and run it to make sure you have entered the expression correctly. Close the query.

   d. Use the Report Wizard to create a report using all of the fields from the query except Order ID. Group the report by Order Date. Sort the fields in each group alphabetically by Company Name. Create a summary to display the total number of units of product ordered per month and the Invoice total for each month.

   e. Use the Stepped layout, Landscape orientation, and the Corporate style. Name the report Orders Report.

   f. View the report. Switch to Report Design View and resize and realign controls as necessary. Format the sums of the invoice totals as currency. Format all four calculated text boxes with a medium font weight, dark blue fore color (8388608), and a raised 2 pt. border.

   g. Drag the Page Footer downward slightly to increase the size of the group footer (Order Date) section and thus increase the space between the group footer and the report footer.

   h. Complete any other formatting, layout, and alignment changes you think are necessary, save them, and close the report.

interactivity (continued)

Build Your Skills (continued)

i. Open the Orders Query in Design View. Enter criteria to display only orders placed in May. Use the wildcard character (*) for the day, to instruct the program to select all order dates in May of 2001. Press Enter and run the query. Access will insert the Like operator. All entries that match the pattern 5/*/01 or 5/*/2001 (depending on which Short Date format your system is using) will be extracted. Save the change to the query design and close the query.

j. Open the Orders Report and view the change. You have created a report for only the month of May. Change the title for the report to May Orders Report. Save and close the report. Rename the report in the Database window.

3. Create Mailing Labels:

a. Use the Label wizard and fields from the Customers table in the Office Furniture database to create mailing labels for the billing department. Use the Avery 5095 label.

b. Use the Arial font with a medium weight in a 10 pt. size. Create the prototype label with the correct spacing and punctuation. Sort the labels alphabetically by the company name and keep the default name for the report.

Problem Solving Exercises

1. Open the Magazine Preferences database. Use the Report Wizard to create a report using the Age, Gender, Occupation and # of Magazines Read Regularly fields. Group the report by age. Click the Grouping Options button to open the Grouping Intervals dialog box. Click the list arrow on the Grouping Intervals list box and select 10s on the drop-down list. This will group the report into age group blocks of 10 years. Do not select a sorting field. Use the Outline 2 layout with a portrait orientation. Use the Casual style and name the report Survey Respondents.

2. View the report. Switch to Report Design View and resize, move and realign the controls appropriately. Open the Grouping and Sorting dialog box and set the Keep Together property so that no age group will be split between two pages of the report. Use the Report Selector to select the report. Use the Auto Format button on the Report Design toolbar to change the style of the report to Bold. View the report in Layout Preview. Decrease the size of the Left and Right page margins to .5 each so that the report fits on two pages.

3. Reformat the report title in any way you choose. You can change the font, font weight, font color, back color, border, special effect, etc. Use both the commands on the Formatting toolbar and the property sheet to achieve a result you are satisfied with. Reformat the Age by 10s text box. Resize the text boxes in the page footer that display the date and page numbers.

4. Add a group footer. Add a calculated control to the group footer to count the number of survey respondents in each age category. Resize and move the controls to the left side of the report aligned with the Age text box and label. Create a border around the calculated control and its label and apply a special effect.

5. Click the AutoFormat button on the Report Design toolbar. Click the Customize button. Select the Create a new AutoFormat based on the Report (report name) radio button. Click OK. The New Style Name dialog box opens. Enter a name for the new format you have just created and click OK. Access will create the new AutoFormat and return you to the AutoFormat dialog box. Your new format is listed in the Report AutoFormats list. You can reuse the design on other reports. Click the Close button. Close the report and save the changes.

glossary

a

Action query

A query that is used to select records and perform operations on them, such as deleting them or placing them in new tables.

Answer Wizard

One of the tabs as part of the Access help feature. Allows you to type a question, and then directs you to the help topics most closely related to your question.

Append Query

A query that adds groups of records from one or more tables to the end of a specified table.

AutoForm

Creates a form automatically from the table or query that you select. You can use AutoForm by selecting it from the New Form dialog box or by clicking the drop-down arrow on the New Object toolbar button.

AutoFormat button

Allows you to open the AutoFormat dialog box, which helps you change the template upon which a form is based; you can choose a template which is predefined or customize your own.

AutoReport

Creates a report automatically from the table or query that you select. You can use AutoReport by selecting it from the New Report dialog box or by clicking the drop-down arrow on the New Object toolbar button.

b

Best Fit

Resizes the width of a column so that it can accommodate the widest entry in the column, including the field name. You can also apply Best Fit by double-clicking the right border of a column's field name.

Bound/Unbound objects

Unbound objects stay the same through every record in a form, while bound objects are linked to particular fields in a database.

c

Cascade Delete Related Records

A command which, when active, ensures that deleting a record from the primary table will automatically delete it from the related table as well.

Cell

The rectangle created by the intersection of a row and a column.

Check box

A small square box that allows you to turn a dialog box option on or off by clicking it.

Clear Layout button

Allows you to eliminate relationships between tables, but does not eliminate just one relationship.

Click

To press and release a mouse button in one motion; usually refers to the left mouse button.

Close button

A button at the top-right corner of every window and box which appears in Microsoft Office. It automatically closes that particular window or box.

Column

A vertical grouping of cells that contains the values for a single field in a database table.

Combo box

A lookup list which is added to a form rather than a table.

Contents

One of the tabs as part of the Access help features. Once clicked this tab displays the contents of the Access help feature.

Controls

The functions in databases which control the data which is presented. Editing these controls changes the way data functions are performed and the way data is represented.

Criteria

Conditions you set that instruct Access to select certain records for a query or filter.

Crosstab query

Query which performs calculations and presents data in a spreadsheet format. It displays one type of data listed down the left side and other types of data across the top.

Custom help

Allows you to provide customized advice and tips which can help someone using the form you create.

d

Data

The fields, values, records, and other information entered and stored in a database.

Data type

Allows you to specify and limit what kinds of data Access will accept in a particular field.

Database

A system for storing, organizing, and retrieving information.

Database management system (DBMS)

Permits you to create a database, and then edit and manipulate its elements.

Database toolbar

Contains graphical buttons which execute specific commands when clicked.

Database window

The main control center for building and working with an Access database. Displays the database object buttons.

Datasheet

Displays the data from a table, form, or query in tabular form.

Datasheet View

Displays the table as it was created in Design View.

Default value

A field property that automatically enters an assigned value into a field for every record.

Delete Query

A query which deletes a group of records from a specified table.

Delete Rows button

A command which allows you to delete a row from your table by clicking this button.

Design grid

The Design View grid in which you create a query or advanced filter.

Design View

The window in which you create and edit a database object.

Dialog box

A box that explains the available command options for you to review or change before executing a command.

Drag

To hold down the mouse button while moving the mouse.

Dynaset

A table which is generated from a select query, it is dynamically linked to a source table.

Enforce Referential Integrity

A command which ensures that for each record in the primary table, there is at least one corresponding record in the related table.

Export

Allows you to save database objects into other databases to be used there.

Expression

A mathematical equation or other form of data control which makes data entry more efficient.

Expression Builder

A dialog box offering you the option of creating a preselected expression or put an expression together yourself using the values presented.

Field

A column of information in a database table that contains a specific type of information.

Field list box

The small window appearing in such places as query Design View and the Relationships window that displays the fields contained in a particular table.

Field properties

Characteristics that control how a field appears, what kinds of data will be accepted in a field, and how that data will be formatted.

Field selector

The gray bar at the top of each datasheet column that contains the field name. Clicking the field selector selects the entire field.

Field size

A field property that limits the number of characters you can enter in a field.

Filter

Criteria you set that Access uses to find and display certain records.

Filter by Form

Command which allows you to select several different criteria from different tables to use to filter your table.

Filter Excluding Selection command

A filter which, when applied, searches for every record which does not include the data you have specified.

Find

Allows you to locate specific types of data or specific records in a database by searching for criteria which you specify.

Form

A database object that often serves as the main user interface for a database. It organizes records so that they are easy to work with.

Form View

The view in which you work with a form, entering and editing records.

Format

The layout of the database, including elements like fonts, sizes, styles, and dimensions. It is changeable and affects the way the entire database appears.

g

Get External Data submenu

Appears on the File menu, and allows you to bring data from an external source into your Access database.

h

Hide/Unhide columns

Command literally hides, or unhides, columns in Datasheet View. Hidden columns and the data contained in them are not seen in the datasheet.

i

Icon

A small graphic that identifies a button or an object.

Import

Allows you to select database objects from other databases and bring them into a new one.

Index

One of the tabs as part of the Access help feature. Allows you to type in a key word, and then directs you to a help topic which matches the keyword you typed.

Input Mask Wizard

Limits the type of data which can be entered into a field by automatically entering data into an easily readable and understandable format.

Insert Rows button

A command which allows you to insert a row into a table by clicking this button.

Insertion point

A vertical blinking line that indicates where text and graphics will be inserted. The insertion point also indicates where an action will begin.

j

Junction table

A table which has a one-to-many relationship with two other tables, it is required when creating a many-to-many relationship with a third table.

l

Label

A box describing the data of the text box attached to it.

Label Wizard

A set of dialog boxes which lead you through a series of steps ending in the creation of a prototypical label for your personal or business correspondence.

Landscape Orientation

A particular style of page orientation which creates a report on a page so that the width is greater than the height.

Link Tables

A command which allows you to create a link in your current database to a table in another database.

List box

A box from which you can choose from a number of options.

Logical operators

Operators that allow you to connect multiple simple conditions in a select query.

Lookup Wizard

A way of creating a list box which allows you to look up the data which fits into the field you add the lookup list to.

m

Mail Merge

A function which allows you to combine the fields and data from an Access database with an MS Word document.

Magnifying tool

Allows you to take a closer look at a page in Print Preview, it is controlled by the mouse and acts as the mouse pointer when in Print Preview mode.

Make-Table query

A query which uses some of the records from one or more tables or queries to create a new table.

Match Case

A command used during the Find command, forces Access to match the capitalization of the specified search field.

Maximize

To enlarge a window to its maximum size. Maximizing an application window causes it to fill the screen; maximizing a database window causes it to fill the application window.

Menu

A list of related commands.

Menu bar

Lists the names of menus containing Access commands. Click a menu name on the menu bar to display a list of commands.

Minimize

To shrink a window to its minimum size. Minimizing an application window reduces it to a button on the taskbar; minimizing a database window reduces it to a short title bar in the application window.

Mouse pointer

The arrow-shaped cursor on the screen that you control by guiding the mouse on your desk. You use the mouse to select and drag items, choose commands, and start or exit programs. The shape of the mouse pointer can change depending on the task being executed.

Move handle

In Design View, the large black square in the upper-left corner of a selected item. Drag the move handle to place the object in a new location.

Multiple Pages display

A mode of Print Preview which allows you to view your document as it will be seen on multiple pages. You may decide to make changes and view the effect it will have on the way the document will appear on the pages when it is printed.

Navigation buttons

The row of buttons at the bottom of a table or form used to move among records.

Object

One of the six main components of a database created in Access. Tables, queries, forms, reports, macros, modules, and pages are all database objects.

Office Assistant

An animated representation of the Microsoft Office 2000 help facility. The Office Assistant provides hints, instruction, and a convenient interface between the user and Access' various help features.

Office Links submenu

Another command which allows you to publish parts of or whole database objects in MS Word, and a Mail Merge may be created from this submenu.

Operators

Symbols and words used to express conditions for selection criteria in a query.

Option button

An object which allows you to make it easier to add a "yes" or "no" entry into a field.

Option group

An object which frames together several options for a particular field, used to limit the amount of options the user may choose from.

Page Breaks

A type of control which effects the way reports are printed, they may be placed anywhere in the report.

Page Setup

A dialog box allowing you to change the dimensions and the layout of what your database objects will look like on the printed page.

Parameter query

A query which is flexible and will prompt you to enter selection criteria every time the query is used.

Properties button

A button on the Formatting toolbar that opens the Properties dialog box, which allows you to change selected field or control properties

Primary key

A field that contains a unique and constant value for each record and can therefore be used as the common field in linked tables.

Print Preview

A view that shows how an object will appear when printed on paper. Useful for evaluating the layout of an object before printing it.

q

Query

A database object that uses a set of instructions you provide to retrieve and display specific data from tables and other queries.

r

Record

A row in a datasheet composed of all the field data for an individual entry.

Record selector

Clicking this gray box at the left edge of a datasheet record highlights the entire record.

Relational database

A database that contains multiple tables that can be linked to one another.

Relationship

The join created between two or more tables using common fields.

Remove Filter button

Undoes the filter which had previously been applied to your table, and shows all the records which appear in the table.

Repair

A function performed on a database when the database is damaged and is performing unpredictably.

Report

A database object that arranges and formats data specifically for printing.

Resizing pointer

At the edges of windows the mouse pointer turns into a double-headed arrow which is used to change the size of the window by dragging it to the desired size.

Restore button

A button on the upper-right side of a window or box. Once you have maximized or minimized it, this button restores it to its original size.

Restore data

When data is lost, the data which comprises the backup copy, must be used to replace, or restore the lost data.

Right-click

To click the right mouse button; often used to access specialized menus and shortcuts.

Row

The horizontal grouping of data fields that forms a record in a datasheet.

Run

The command that activates a query.

s

Save As

Command in the File menu, which allows you to save documents in different files and folders, and in different modes, such as saving a form as a report.

ScreenTip

A brief description of a button or other item that appears when the mouse pointer is paused over it. Other ScreenTips are accessed by using the What's This? feature on the Help menu or by clicking the question mark button in a dialog box.

Scroll arrows

Appear at either end of the scroll bar box. Click them to scroll the scroll bar up or down to view the database you are looking at.

Scroll bar

A graphical device for moving vertically or horizontally through a database object with the mouse. Scroll bars are located along the right and bottom edges of a window.

Scroll bar box

A small gray box located inside a scroll bar that indicates your current position relative to the rest of the window. You can advance a scroll bar box by dragging it, clicking the Scroll bar on either side of it, or by clicking the Scroll arrows.

Select query

The most common type of query, used to extract and associate fields from tables and other queries and present this data in datasheet form.

Shortcut key

A keyboard equivalent of a menu command such as [Ctrl]+[S] for Save.

Shortcut menu

A pop-up menu accessed by right-clicking the mouse. The contents of the menu depend on your current activity.

Simple Condition

A single selection criterion which is used to sort records in a query.

Simple Query Wizard

A wizard which allows you to create a simple, select query quickly and easily, by helping you through a series of dialog boxes.

Sizing handles

The small black squares that appear on the border of an item when it is selected. Dragging these handles allows you to resize the object.

Sort order

The direction in which records are organized (i.e. ascending or descending).

Sorting and Grouping dialog box

Allows you to set the sorting order of fields and determine whether a field is used to group data in a report.

Specific record box

The box in the bottom left corner of a datasheet or form that indicates the number of the active record.

SQL query

A query created using the Structured Query Language, the basic programming language Access uses to create and perform queries.

Status bar

The gray bar at the bottom of the window that provides information about your current activity in Access and displays the field descriptions you entered in Design View.

Structured Query Language (SQL)

Programming language used by Access to create and execute queries.

Subform

A way of embedding one form into another form, the subform displays related records to the main form.

t

Tab Order

The direction in which the insertion point will move through the fields of a database object when hitting the Tab key.

Table

The object that gives a database its basic structure, storing its records and fields in tabular form.

Template

A preconstructed database. Allows you to take a database which already has its basic outline, and fill it in with your own data.

Text box

A box containing data which is text rather than objects or images.

Title bar

The horizontal bar at the top of the window that displays the name of the document or application that appears in the window.

Toggle button

An object which simulates the pressing of a button, which may be used for fields which have a "yes" or "no" type entry.

Toolbar

A graphical bar containing buttons that act as shortcuts for common commands.

Toolbox

A toolbar that contains items you can add to a form or report in Design View.

u

Update Query

A query which makes complete, uniform changes to records in one or more tables.

v

Validation Rule

A rule that determines the type of data that is acceptable in a database.

Validation Text

Lets the user know that the Validation Rule has been violated, and what type of data will be accepted into the database.

Value

The data that you place in a field.

w

What's This?

A help feature that allows you to click a screen item in order to receive a ScreenTip that explains the item.

Wildcard characters

Symbols that represent unknown letters or numbers when using the Find feature.

Wizard

A series of specialized dialog boxes that walks you through the completion of certain tasks.

z

Zoom

A command used in Print Preview mode while the cursor appears in the shape of a magnifying glass, allows you to take a closer look at the document in Print Preview mode.

index

The table below summarizes the external data files that have been provided for the student. Many of the exercises in this book cannot be completed without these files. The files are distributed as part of the Instructor's Resource Kit and are also available for download at http://www.mhhe.com/it/cit/index.mhtml. Please note that the table below only lists the raw files that are provided, not the versions students are instructed to save after making changes to the raw files or new files that the students create themselves. Once introduced, some files are used throughout the book.

Lesson	Skill Name/Page #	File Name	Introduced In
Lesson 1	Opening an Existing Database/AC 1.2	Office Furniture Inc	do it! step 4
	Opening an Existing Database/AC 1.3	Home Video Collection	Practice
	Editing Records in a Datasheet/AC 1.15	acprac1-7.doc	Practice
	Interactivity/AC 1.25	Recipes	Build Your Skills #1
	Interactivity/AC 1.26	Pepper Sirloin Steak.doc	Build Your Skills #5
	Interactivity/AC 1.26	Chocolate Turtle Cheescake.doc	Build Your Skills #5
Lesson 2	Using the Table Wizard/AC 2.7	Tuning Tracker	Practice
	Establishing Table Relationships/AC 2.16	Employees 2	do it! step 1
Lesson 3	Creating an AutoForm/AC 3.3	Tuning Tracker 2	Practice
	Entering Records Using a Form/AC 3.21	acprac3-8.doc	Practice
Lesson 4	No new files		